A child can see all of eternity
in a grain of sand.

paraphrased from William Blake
Auguries of Innocence

To Wendy

With warm personal

regards

Fay Hartzen

Raymond H. Hartjen, Ph.D.

Empowering the Child

Nurturing the Hungry Mind

*Elementary Education
for the 21st Century*

Alternative Education Press, Ltd.
Post Office Box 265
Port Tobacco, Maryland 20677

Alternative Education Press, Ltd.
P.O. Box 265
Port Tobacco, MD 20677

Printed in the United States of America

Library of Congress Cataloging Card Number 94-94527

ISBN 1-885599-00-5

Alternative Education Press, Ltd. books are available at special discounts for bulk purchases for sales promotions, premiums, fundraising, or educational use. For details, contact:

Special Sales Director
Alternative Education Press, Ltd.
P.O. Box 265
Port Tobacco, MD 20677

To

Lisa and Anne

whose very existence sustains me

Acknowledgments

This book could not have been written without the base of knowledge I gained during what might be termed my Pittsburgh years, 1965 to 1973. These were rich in educational experiences. My second child was born there, and my first daughter was ready for some form of schooling. I was employed as a research associate at what I perceived to be a think tank of educational research, the Learning Research and Development Center, and spent many hours videotaping children at work and play in varied educational settings. My mentors, Robert Glaser, Lauren Resnick, Leo Klopfer and others, had far more faith in me than I had in myself. Their strict adherence to school improvement through research stood in sharp contrast with the more intuitive approach used by those promoting the open classroom where our daughters were first introduced to self-initiated learning. The Shady Lane School became our first contact with open education. Here, among others, Nancy Carbonara stands out as the teacher who helped my daughter Lisa and me make the transition to self-initiated learning, while Nancy Currey at the model school of the School of Health-Related Professions at the University of Pittsburgh was daughter Anne's first teacher and my second.

There were individuals, such as Reverend Stewart and Julie Pierson, who became close friends as well as colleagues on the board of directors of the Shady Lane School, where I had the good fortune of working on serious school problems with other board members and the dedicated staff of the school.

There was also close collaboration with the faculty of Chatham College, which had assumed responsibility for some of the region's first summer workshops on open education. It was through these workshops that Mary Corbett was helped over the transition from traditional to open education as she took charge of one of the first open classrooms in the city of Pittsburgh school system at Starrett School. The process of working with other parents, teachers and school administrators of Starrett School was enlightening and rewarding.

The resulting interaction with Mary Mullino and June Delano in the Pittsburgh schools' central office led to my being engaged by them as they conceived and brought into being their upper elementary magnet open classroom center.

I am also indebted to my former wife, Andrea, for spearheading our linkages with the schools that embraced our daughters. Seeing these environments through another's eyes added greatly to my understanding of the underlying dynamics.

Moving on to the present, you, the readers, are the beneficiaries of my editor, Tamia Karpeles, who has done a masterful job of paring away irrelevant issues, reorganizing material, and pointing out breaks that needed smoother transitions. I have gained much in writing proficiency through the editor-author relationship. The other very significant person in the creation of this book has been my administrative assistant, Helen Joseph, who, through her computer, looked to the minutest detail as the book took shape over time.

Now, there are the readers, these friends and colleagues who have taken their personal time to read the text and comment on its strengths and weaknesses. Two have been especially meticulous in the scrutiny of the text: Margaret Nold, who used her free time while on watch as she sailed north for two weeks with her father from Florida to South Carolina, and Leo Karpeles, who has written pages of comments and questions.

A special thanks is due Barbara Mullins, the University of Maryland Prince George's County student-teacher coordinator, who, reading earlier chapters, strongly encouraged me to move forward with haste.

My other readers—Andrea Grant, my former wife; Lisa and Anne, my daughters; and Judy McKnight, a colleague in the National Diffusion Network—have provided many insights that were very helpful.

I would like to express my deep appreciations to principal Emily Stephenson-Green and the teachers of the Irwin Avenue School, who generously opened their minds and their classrooms to me for videotaping and observation during the fall of 1993.

And finally, I would like to thank Bob Gabrys of the Maryland State Department of Education for the suggestion that I explore and document the self-initiated learning school culture.

Preface

I have been very impressed with children's enthusiasm for learning in open/progressive education settings, but I felt this movement needed a convincing rationale to turn the heads of a population steeped in traditional education. So I set out to create a framework that would enable everyone to understand more fully the dynamics of how children learned in this new (old) environment. I accomplished this task by exploring, prospecting, if you will, for gems of ideas from noneducational, nontraditional sources such as Erich Fromm, Richard Leakey, Mitchell Waldrop, Stephen Covey, Rollo May and others. I found exciting ideas that gave broad insights that have led to the formation of a philosophical rationale for self-initiated learning.

An equally powerful motivation was the restructuring movement that is sweeping across our nation's schools. Individual schools are being empowered to rethink how they are educating their charges. Instructional support teams, with memberships drawn from faculties, parents, administrators, and the business communities, are now being empowered to redesign their schools' curricula and overriding philosophy. It appeared to me that there may be a big knowledge gap in the makeup of these teams. Not only did they have to catch up on all of the best and latest in traditional education, but, if they were to take a major leap forward to meet the needs of the twenty-first century, they would have to have some convincing, eye-opening documents to provide a rationale for a change of some magnitude. It was with this prod that I decided to write this book. It will, hopefully, awaken some to a new age of education. My goal is not to create a new fad but to replant the seed for the exploration of a fully-expanding educational experience for our youth.

Contents

Part 1
Background

Chapter 1
The rationale underlying a new philosophy of education

Chapter 2
A review of various dimensions of self-initiated learning supported in part through four vignettes depicting the adaptability of children

Chapter 3
A review of how we continue to follow the Horace Mann principles of education

Chapter 1
Underlying Rationale and Overview

Every so often, we rediscover a certain form of learning. For a while, it brings a flourish of excitement to the classroom—then it falters and dies.

It is a form of learning that helps students fully realize their own potential. It draws on children's unique ability to explore and discover. It is predominantly self-initiated, and once begun, it develops its own momentum. Again and again, it has transformed children who would not learn in the past. With so many individual successes, why is this self-initiated form of learning repeatedly abandoned?

I have searched to answer this question. I believe the failure lies not in the method, but in ourselves. We fail to recognize its intrinsic value, fail to retrain our teachers in its use, and fail to admit that this form of education's central tenet strikes at the very heart of how children learn and retain most effectively.

I was deeply involved with self-initiated learning during the late sixties and early seventies. My two daughters were enrolled in progressive classrooms at that time, while I was serving both as a consultant to the Pittsburgh City schools and as a board member of the Shady Lane School, a leading school in the movement. Although the trend toward a progressive learning system has since lost popular support, I have never been able to dismiss its significance.

In 1991, I met with Bob Gabrys, who was investigating innovative learning programs for Maryland schools that scored poorly in performance tests. He asked me about my experiences with self-initiated learning, and I told him about Justin.

When Justin came to the Pittsburgh magnet school where I served as consultant, he had been earmarked as a potential dropout. His mother had to pry him out of bed each morning, force-feed him his breakfast, and press his lunch in his hands as she pushed him out the door.

Several months after his enrollment there, she stopped me at church one day and said, "I can't believe the change in Justin! He's getting up early and fixing his own breakfast and lunch so he can catch the first bus to school. He greets his teachers as they arrive in the morning, and they have to push him out when they lock up in the afternoon."

Justin exemplified self-initiated learning at its most successful. When I related this story to Bob, his response was immediate: Document how this form of education works, and let's use it.

So I went home and dusted off the books.

The way to begin, I assumed, was by revisiting the works of authors who spearheaded the last major movement in self-initiated learning. But I soon discovered that these books could only tell me what I already knew. Because of my long-term professional involvement in education, because of the testimony I see today in my daughters as they enter with confidence into their adult careers, I already believe in the progressive movement. There had to be something more, something forceful enough to convince educators, parents, and politicians that it is time to revise our teaching methods across the board.

I began to look elsewhere, in books that would not immediately be regarded as sources for educational reform. From Richard Leakey's *Origins Reconsidered: In Search of What Makes Us Human*, to M. Mitchell Waldrop's *Complexity*, to Stephen R. Covey's *The Seven Habits of Highly Effective People*, I began to review contemporary thought across a range of human considerations.

My prime reading time was in the evening, often in bed. I might cover only a few pages, or I might find myself carried away into the small hours of morning, following an elusive connection between my search and the author's argument. Often I would read myself to sleep, only to wake abruptly a few hours later with a sudden insight clearly relevant to education.

One of my most arresting insights came from computer-generated birds.

In *Complexity*, Waldrop describes a workshop that took place in Los Alamos, New Mexico, back in 1987. The theme was artificial life, and Craig Reynolds, an expert in computer animation, presented a program he had developed in which simulated birds learned to fly in formation.

To do this, Reynolds wrote the simplest program possible, containing only three rules. He instructed his animated birds (dubbed *boids*) to (1) maintain a discreet distance from all other objects, (2) try to match the speed of nearby boids, and (3) continually migrate toward the densest areas of boid population.

Reynolds turned his boids loose within a computer-generated obstacle course. Obedient to his rules, they soon organized from random patterns into a well-defined flock. Moreover, they maintained this formation even as they avoided the objects that they encountered. This was remarkable. The program's instructions never addressed the behavior of flocks, but only the behavior of individual boids. Their ability to form and maintain their flight pattern was not *defined* by the program—it *emerged* from it. In other words, those three parameters were sufficient for the boids to learn to do this task on their own, without additional instructions.

Reynolds' computer simulation uses a "bottom-up" approach to programming. A traditional "top-down" program contains thousands of individual statements that define exactly what will happen under any possible circumstance. Bottom-up programming simply creates broad parameters from which the desired outcome can emerge. It is faster, ties up less memory in the computer, and still contains all the necessary information for success.

It suddenly occurred to me that we have been programming students from the top down for years. Our schools feed everyone the same rigid set of data. This produces students who function on the most literal level. They are taught to memorize reams of information, but they are never given a framework for solving their own problems. The first obstacle that appears in their paths is likely to knock them down.

Alternatively, you can give students a few guidelines to build on from the bottom up. Suddenly you free them to explore on their own. They learn how to learn—a skill they will draw upon for the rest of their lives.

You can see an example of this at the River East School, part of the Center for Collaborative Education in New York City, where they have established ten essentials of learning: children there explore the principles of basic literacy, math skills that focus on logic and problem-solving, and self-expression through writing, art, and verbal communication. They also master thinking skills, independent learning, socialization, and the ability to love themselves and their efforts. It is a curriculum that has proven itself over time.

Believing that children can only realize their full potential in a bottom-up educational setting, I began to contemplate the fewest parameters that could be used to define the progressive classroom.

I eventually came up with four simple rules, which I believe could serve as the basis for all elementary education and possibly for life itself.

Rule 1: Support the establishment of long-term attending skills in young children. (Chapter 5)

The ability to focus on a task for an extended period is crucial to any child's development. This skill will be a valuable asset, not only during the school years, but throughout the child's life. By providing guidance and modeling, teachers and older students help the child choose a task and learn to stick with it.

Rule 2:   Support, focus and shape self-initiating behaviors in young children. (Chapter 6)

Self-initiation is another key to being successful in life, yet traditional schools do not allow this talent to emerge. When children leave school and begin to function as adults, their success depends on their ability to take the initiative in everything they do, from finding work to building a relationship. Nothing is accomplished in the self-initiated learning environment without the student making it happen. To lay the foundation for this success, the progressive classroom must encourage and support all aspects of self-initiated behavior.

Rule 3:   Enable students to become fluent in all forms of thinking skills through daily use and practice. (Chapter 7)

The honing and refinement of thinking skills lies at the very heart of this free micro-society. Both thinking and negotiating skills are essential to self-initiated learning. Much contemporary research focuses on thinking skills in the classroom. We need to develop a means for applying these findings in the progressive educational setting.

Rule 4:   Enable students to explore varied avenues of creativity and encourage them to develop proficiency in at least one. (Chapter 8)

In his book The Sane Society, *Erich Fromm contends that a tension exists within all of us between creativeness and destructiveness. By encouraging students to explore their innate creative potential, we help them to master dormant destructive tendencies. This, in turn, minimizes behavioral problems and promotes constructive activities.*

These are my four basic rules for empowering students to open their own doors of educational opportunity. To be effective, they must be accompanied by environmental changes designed to support students' natural inquisitiveness.

Current research has found that students do better in small, caring schools. Recent trends show that large schools are increasingly broken down into smaller units, giving students and teachers alike the opportunity to know each other better. Only in this sociable environment can a school become a caring community. This school community, in turn, nurtures and hones the interactive social skills that are a distinguishing feature of successful people. (Chapter 4)

So how do we begin to implement such a transition within our traditional educational system? Again, I found insight in *Complexity*, through the analogy of phase transition—the molecular alterations that affect some substances as they change temperature.

Water can exist as a solid, in the form of ice, as a liquid, or as a gas. The transition from one state to the other takes place in a moment and is called phase change. There is only a single-order phase change in the state of water.

There are substances, however, that undergo what's called a second-order phase transition. At low temperatures, such a substance will crystallize into a form that is essentially solid. Warmed, it changes to a liquid. But in between, there is a range in which the substance can be both solid and liquid. When it begins to warm from its rigid, crystalline state, the substance takes on the characteristics of continental masses broken by lakes. As it moves toward its liquid state, the continents become islands, the lakes become seas. In theory, the substance can achieve a point, in the middle stages of this phase transition, that represents a balance between order—the rigid state—and chaos, the liquid state.

I gradually came to apply this phase transition concept as a model for educational institutions. An educational system with a well-established infrastructure exists in a state analogous to early phase transition, where continents exist with a few lakes. In this state it is virtually impossible to bring about change: rigid infrastructure locks the entire system together.

I realized that as we restructure our schools, we push them through a sort of phase transition until they take on the characteristics of many islands, with shorelines in a constant state of fluctuation. Only in this flexible state, midway between order and chaos, can progressive change occur.

When we think of our schools as islands, we see that the adaptability of each island's shoreline makes this structure more responsive to the realities of a world that constantly changes, a world made up of individuals with very different needs. Certainly, every island, or school, is more vulnerable under these conditions. Weak islands may disappear, but strong ones will flourish, their shorelines stabilizing, even growing over time.

To push the phase transition of our schools toward this balanced, flexible state, we must begin by decentralizing power, shifting it from away from the main office, away from the cadre of superintendents and administrators, and placing it instead in the hands of the teachers, parents, principals, and the individual school communities they create.

As schools now exist, teachers are powerless to react, moment by moment, to the situations that arise in their classrooms. Under such conditions, how can a teacher respond to the unique needs of an individual student? Being freed from the infrastructure of the larger organization gives individual schools and individual teachers an opportunity to try out new ideas. Throughout the history of formal education, beginning with John Dewey's influential movement toward progressive education in 1910, one can find examples of such schools that worked, and many of them are still working today. Here are a few examples:

- The City and Country School, founded by Caroline Pratt in 1914

- The Irwin Avenue School in Charlotte, North Carolina, founded in 1972

- The English Infant School, which was translated in America as open education in the period circa 1965-1974

- The Reggio Emilia School in Northern Italy, founded in 1963

- The St. Paul's Community School project, organized by Wayne Jennings in 1992

- The Coalition of Essential Schools at Brown University, which instituted a problem-centered curriculum in 1984, undertaking the seemingly impossible task of introducing this method at the high school level

- The Center for Collaborative Education in New York City, founded in 1988

- The Oruaiti School, which operated in the northernmost province of New Zealand from 1960 to 1968

Such movements may falter or fail simply by losing popular support. Yet you can talk to children and adults across the generations who were fortunate enough to experience progressive education in settings where the methodology worked well. For them, self-initiated learning is an experiment that they will draw upon throughout their lives.

Children have remarkable inner resources, representing a power which can be used for great achievements. When we empower them through self-initiated learning, we enable them to tap into this power, releasing limitless energies. Suddenly the children assume ownership of the task of learning, and our roles are relegated to that of facilitators and guides. In the wake of this strategy, motivational problems cease to exist. Behavioral problems, such as acting out, poor attendance and noncompliance, all vanish. Teachers will still have to rein in their students' high spirits at times, but this means rechanneling exuberance into productive lines, which can be done with subtle rules established through deliberate collaboration between teachers and students. How much better than simply stifling a student's natural reactions to restriction!

We have programmed children from the top down for centuries. Today's children deserve to experience bottom-up, rule-based education. They have proven themselves highly adaptable to the variety of artificial educational environments which we adults create. It is our challenge now to establish an environment that will teach children to take command of their own learning experience. The children are not the cause of today's crisis in education. Rather, the cause lies with an adult infrastructure that has become land-bound and rigid. We must establish a new commitment to education, founded on faith in our children's ability to strike out on their own. And we will begin by approaching the changing shoreline that lies nearer to the edge of chaos.

I have reexamined my own experiences and interviewed others who felt that they or their children flourished in the open classroom environment. I have visited the schools and talked with the teachers. I have drawn on my contacts as the State Facilitator for the National Diffusion Network in Maryland. As such, I have been exposed to many of the latest changes in education. It is from these experiences that I have reached some unexpected conclusions. Now I hope to bring new insights to an old way of learning.

Consider this book a starting point. Here is a broad rationale that could carry education into the twenty-first century. Whether or how we use this rationale to end the current crisis in learning is up to you and me.

Chapter 2
Background and Characteristics of a Self-Initiated Learning Classroom

I greatly admire those insightful educators who, taking a leap of faith, brought their version of the English Infant School to America, establishing what became known as open/progressive education (O/PE). They created a learning environment that began with children's natural inquisitiveness, fostered good social development, and honed their thinking skills. Thanks largely to their initiative, in the early seventies my wife and I sent our two preschool-age daughters into the arms of a cluster of loving teachers. Our commitment to self-initiated learning was one of the most important decisions we ever made in our children's education.

It saddens me that the open classroom concept became just another fad. Architects have reduced the concept to nothing more than physical structure, a cost-saving way to build big schools. Today, the term *open classroom* is applied to any classroom without partitioned spaces—a type of structure that is totally inappropriate for the style of teaching taking place there.

For my family, the O/PE movement was equivalent to the *aha* of a scientific breakthrough. It was an entirely new way of thinking about how to educate youngsters. I believe that many of today's learning innovations are rooted in that abandoned movement. The problem is that these O/PE elements are being implemented in a piecemeal fashion, which accomplishes little. Only by exerting all our efforts in the same direction, bringing about a totally new model for the classroom, can we realize a major benefit for today's children.

In his book *The Seven Habits of Highly Effective People*, Stephen R. Covey talks about a paradigm shift, in which a person's entire perspective is reconfigured as a whole. In such a case, the results are far greater than the sum of the parts. Likewise, when the O/PE movement took hold, it involved the parents, the school, and the community. The total reorientation of our teachers took place in a single summer, and besides being exhilarating and energizing, it had a tremendous impact.

Today, however, the innovative components— interdisciplinary learning, cooperative learning, thinking skills, and the like—simply do not add up to the sum of the parts that existed in the open classroom. Today's components fail to excite children so that they would eagerly meet their teachers as they enter the school. Today's components do not motivate children to write fifteen pages when they can get away with five.

When competent teachers were given free reign, our children also took great leaps forward. Working in self-disciplined classrooms, the children became highly focused; they produced lengthy papers, along with other significant projects. The children were coming alive as their natural inquisitiveness was rekindled. But then, as now, standardized tests were the measure by which one judged the success of an educational endeavor. And open classroom children, coming from a situation that did not emphasize testing, often did not do well. These poor showings helped to speed the demise of this movement.

In fact, standardized tests simply can't measure the type of skills in which the O/PE child becomes proficient. A new trend today is toward annual performance tests which attempt to measure a child's ability to cope with practical problems. These tests gauge not only the unique skills of individuals, but also their ability to perform with and contribute to a group.

Forward-thinking educators believe that performance behaviors are true indicators of a child's real-world potential. Ironically, traditional classroom teachers now must modify their teaching styles, reemphasizing such O/PE concepts as integrated learning and thinking skills, to enable their students to perform well on these tests.

The Irwin Avenue School in Charlotte, North Carolina has been operating on the open classroom model since the early seventies. The teachers are well-trained, and the model works efficiently while serving an inner city population that is 40 percent African-American and Hispanic. It would be interesting to see performance test results from this school. These students are achieving at grade level, as they must in order to keep the school operating as a magnet center.

What was there in the O/PE classroom that does not exist today? What made this movement so revolutionary that children actually became excited about education? What have we turned our backs on?

Respecting Children as Independent Learners

One difference lies in the way we treat children as learners. Conventional educators have based our modern school system on premises that don't work: a premise that children will become educated if they can just hold their attention long enough; a premise that they can systematically feed all the components of learning to a child and produce an educated youngster. The problem is that children generally don't cooperate. They want something more. And I believe that "something more" is *respect as learners*. Children want their teachers and parents to exhibit faith in their natural inquisitiveness.

Faith in our children's abilities as independent inquirers is perhaps the single most important dimension of the O/PE classroom. We support this faith by respecting children as they undertake their chosen projects. Erich Fromm, in his book *The Art of Loving*, suggests that this respect, or faith, is the essential element in helping children realize their potential:

> The presence of this faith makes the difference between education and manipulation. Education is identical with helping the child realize his potentialities. The opposite of education is manipulation, which is based on the absence of faith in the growth of potentialities, and on the conviction that a child will be right only if the adults put into him what is desirable

and suppress what seems to be undesirable. There is no need of faith in the robot, since there is no life in it either. (P. 112)

Similarly, in *The Seven Habits of Highly Effective People*, Covey talks about the objectives he and his wife had unthinkingly placed on their own son. As the boy failed miserably to meet those objectives, they became aware of the pressures they had placed on him and managed to withdraw their imposed goals. The child, given a little space, began to blossom along the lines best suited to his own interests and desires.

In *The Prophet*, Kahlil Gibran compares the role of the parent/teacher to that of a bow. Its objective is to shoot straight and hard, but the bow must release the arrow to its own fate as it moves through space.

When students are given the opportunity to choose tasks that interest them, there is no stopping them. You will see this time and again in self-initiated learning, where it is the mode for students to work on material and projects that they choose. You will find groups of students who focus on a specific topic and stay with it for months on end. This runs counter to the recurring lament we hear from today's teachers, who say that the total attention span of children is no more than fifteen to twenty minutes. Yet in the O/PE classroom, one of the first objectives of the progressive teacher is to help a student or group of students find a project that is of keen interest and encourage them to stay focused on it for an extended period. The key to successful inquiry, such focused behavior enables a child to remain attentive to a task in spite of the commotion that might be forthcoming from others in the classroom.

The Self-Controlled Behavior of Children

This leads to one of the most impressive dimensions of self-initiated learning: the behavior of the children. No one is out of control. Once given the opportunity to choose projects in their area of interest, children can stay on task. The locus of discipline shifts from the teacher to the children, who become self-disciplined even without consciously controlling their impulses. Far from practicing overt restraint, the children are openly enjoying themselves. When children are given the freedom to control their learning environment, they become essentially self-governing, exploring the world within the rules that they themselves have established with the guidance of their teacher. A child who goes out of bounds will be challenged by the other children; if that does not work, the inappropriate behavior is addressed during a group meeting in which all parties are encouraged to discuss their differences, and the children work as a community to find a solution.

In the third grade, my daughter Lisa attended a semi-open classroom. One day, after some isolated incident of misconduct on the playground, the teacher instituted a general punishment, denying all the children access to the drinking fountain. Lisa considered this unjust. Being something of a renegade, she organized a protest. The children secretly worked together to create protest posters, and just before dismissal, on signal, they stood up and marched around the room chanting, "No water, no work."

Lisa's teacher related this incident to my wife and me, telling us how she had to fight back a smile as she disciplined the children. I could only think how wrong her actions were. She was wrong not to share her delight with the children. She was wrong not to involve the children in working out the original problem, and she was wrong not to establish a socially interactive environment that allowed social matters to be "curricular" matters.

Improved Social Interactive Behavior of Students

Learning to live with your neighbor is an essential dimension of the O/PE classroom. It prepares students to move into the community. A recent conversation I had with the principal of the Irwin Avenue School demonstrates the impact of naturally-occurring social behavior in the classroom.

As part of their open classroom activities, the Irwin Avenue students perform community service. They had been invited to help deliver Friendship Trays (somewhat similar to Meals on Wheels) to the elderly. The parent coordinator could not help noting the difference in the behavior of the students from Irwin Avenue School as compared with students from more traditional schools. The Irwin Avenue students demonstrated skills of caring, taking turns, and being considerate—not only of their elderly beneficiaries, but also of their peers. They even actively engaged the elderly in conversation. In contrast, students from traditional schools fussed over who would carry the trays, fussed over whose turn it was, and hardly said a word to the recipients.

Consider for a moment how traditional schools deal with social behavior. It generally is not considered part of the curriculum, and even if teachers take the time to explain how social skills are supposed to work, the children are rarely given an opportunity to test these skills on an interactive basis. The exercise is confined to the class period; consequently, the students are not allowed the daily practice necessary to hone these skills.

If students are supposed to be social creatures all of their lives, doesn't it make sense to encourage them to develop social skills in the controlled setting of the classroom?

The Changing Role of the Teacher

In Pittsburgh, I helped establish a pilot O/PE classroom in a traditional school. Before long, an unforeseen problem arose—not with the children in the pilot program, but with the children from the traditional classrooms. When they realized that Mary Corbett's kids were having fun while they were learning, they complained: "Why can't we get our schooling the way Miss Corbett's kids do?" Given a pass to go to the bathroom or run an errand, they would invariably wind up looking in the windows of Mary Corbett's room.

So the O/PE classroom windows were covered up with construction paper. But the problem continued as the children talked with friends who were in Miss Corbett's class. Soon meetings were called to open a dialogue between the parents whose children attended the open classroom, other parents who wanted their kids in one, and parents who didn't want anything to do with any newfangled form of schooling.

Was this problem resolved? Only in the short term. The meetings led to a number of new, partially progressive classrooms, but the effort was half-hearted. The teachers received minimal training, and the classrooms lacked a cohesive commitment to the concept. In the long run, the traditionalists won out. Open classrooms were discontinued after only a few years.

Obviously, the role of the teacher changes drastically in the O/PE classroom. Theodore Sizer, who directs the Coalition of Essential Schools at Brown University, comments on this:

> The governing practical metaphor of the school should be student-as-worker, rather than the more familiar metaphor of teacher-as-deliverer-of-instructional-services. A prominent pedagogy will be coaching, to provoke students to learn how to learn and thus to teach themselves.

Covey also stresses the importance of "learner-controlled instruction" and defines the parameters of this form of learning for adults. Cognitive psychologists, who are discovering numerous dimensions of this form of coaching, recognize it as a powerful tool for fostering thinking skills and long-term learning.

We are constantly uncovering new truths about how children learn best. I believe some of the most recent discoveries would have come to light long ago if the O/PE classroom movement had been maintained as a whole.

The Aging of an Idea

Self-initiated learning is a time-tested concept. It has been practiced in America since the late sixties and existed long before that in England, originating in 1910 with John Dewey and Progressive Education. In New Zealand, it was identified and documented in the late sixties by Elwyn S. Richardson, whose book *In the Early World* should be required reading for every elementary teacher. Quite recently, the Reggio Emilia early-education schools in Italy, working with a child-centered approach modeled closely after Progressive Education, were celebrated through a traveling display that has moved around our country for several years. This model program is well described in *The Hundred Languages of Children*, by Carolyn Edwards, Lella Gandini and George Forman.

Our progress has been slow and frustrating, perhaps because we needed time to mature, to research the concepts of thinking skills and cooperative learning, and to develop methodologies that could help us understand what makes self-initiated learning work.

The bottom line is clear: It's time for a change. Many elements that were barely understood decades ago have now been carefully defined and tested, and today the mood is right for schools to make the change. Traditional schools are known to be outdated and out of touch. Increasingly, parents say they want more for their children. Most of all, industry is crying out for a well-rounded, thinking graduate. Twenty-first century America needs the leap forward that only a progressive classroom can give.

A handful of schools have been graduating students with this advanced form of education for the past twenty years, while the country at large has waited for a holy grail to materialize—but it's been here all along. It's past time for us to acknowledge the potential that arises from such an educational system.

In brief, these are the characteristics that foster self-initiated learning:

- An environment rich in resources, where students can become highly focused and develop long-term attending skills.

- An environment that allows children the freedom to explore their own interests and ideas, an environment that promotes a continuous exchange of ideas.

- Teachers who are trained to act as coach, guide, model thinker, prodder, therapist, moderator, raiser of questions, issues, and alternative perspectives.

- A school that functions as a community of inquiry, a limited democracy where children practice good social skills, good human skills, on a minute-by-minute basis.

- Teachers who are willing to accept the possibility that children can have ideas intellectually beyond their own.

The children have always been ready and able to make the change to such a classroom environment, as you will see.

The Adaptable Child

School settings, teaching styles, and educational philosophies are just a few of the variables defining the environment into which we immerse our children at an early age. If you were to look at the variety of classroom settings these children enter, you would be impressed at their ability to adapt. Some cry on the first day of school; others sit in quiet protest; but most, after a few days, conform to the rules, regulations, and discipline imposed upon them. And, for a while—sometimes weeks, sometimes years—they adjust and learn to be happy about their experience.

This average classroom may be familiar to us, being very similar to what we experienced as children. You will see a group of twenty to thirty youngsters and one adult who is obviously in charge. Yes, there are innovations. The floors may be carpeted, the desks movable. There is more small-group work and better media support. The teacher might use an overhead projector instead of the blackboard, so she can see and talk to the class as she writes or changes transparencies. It is obvious the children have adapted well. They all appear to be attentive and on task.

Vignette 1: Individually Prescribed Instruction

Now, let's look at another classroom. It is the late sixties. You're entering a school thirty miles outside Pittsburgh, in the heart of a blue-collar community—definitely not affluent.

The children are in an Individually Prescribed Instruction (IPI) science class. They work in carrels—desks with high vertical dividers to minimize distractions. The children may be working alone or in pairs. You can hear a low hum in the classroom, yet it's easy to carry on a conversation.

The teacher is engaged with one or two children at her desk. Some are waiting to talk to her, conversing with friends. In an adjacent room, you see shelves of coded boxes. Occasionally, a child will get up and exchange one box for another.

As you peer over the top of a carrel, you observe a child with an assortment of things on her desk. She is making adjustments to a scale, noting her observations in a workbook, and finally writing out her conclusions.

The students are so busy with what they are doing, they are not aware that you've entered the room. You sense activity throughout the class, yet everyone appears to be well disciplined. Where is the source of that discipline?

Lessons in an IPI program form a carefully-sequenced curriculum in which students undertake independent studies according to their scores on a pretest. At the end of the sequence, students take a post-test; with a score of 85 percent or better, they move on to the next series. A student who scores below 85 percent is cycled back through a remedial sequence and given the test again.

This experimental form of instruction was the focus of research at the University of Pittsburgh's Learning Research and Development Center in the late sixties and early seventies. It generated such widespread interest, a film was made available to answer basic questions. As a research associate at the center, studying for my doctorate under Robert Glaser, I sometimes fielded calls from educators, who often asked for information about our "school for exceptional children." The first time I heard this query, I assumed that the caller had contacted the wrong center. In fact, he had simply assumed that the students, being self-directed and focused at their work, must be gifted.

This was not the case. *All* of the students at that school participated in IPI reading, math and science. All of the students adapted to the learning environment established by the research team from the university. The teachers, who had received intensive training, established the parameters within which the children were to operate. And the children, in response, achieved a level of behavior that the uninitiated viewed as gifted and talented.

Vignette 2: An Open Classroom

While I was involved with Pittsburgh's fledgling magnet school, I had an opportunity to visit classrooms modeled after the English Infant School. Here is what I saw and heard as I walked in the front door of the Prospect School in Bennington, Vermont.

As I approached the steps, I came upon several children playing recorders. It was obvious that one knew how to play well, and the others were attempting to emulate her skills. As pleasant tones of the virtuoso contrasted with the approximations of her protégés, the mixture of sound both warmed my heart and sent shivers up my spine, and I smiled as I walked by.

Inside was like nothing I had ever seen before. Chaos! No desks—an old armchair, a rocking chair, racks of books, shelves and shelves of boxes containing bottle caps, wooden cubes, paper and cardboard of all colors and weights, leather, milk cartons, wood, magnets, blocks, nuts and bolts, old radio motors, and the like. Some kids curled up in cubbies reading, others at tables with early versions of what we now call manipulatives (small objects—bottle caps, cubes, dried beans—that a child can use to learn basic math concepts). I saw a table cluttered with balances, microscopes, magnifying glasses, and a sign that said *Science Center*. At first glance I could not find the teacher, but she soon appeared, in long hair and coveralls, with traces of clay on her hands to show that she had been busy demonstrating the pottery craft to a few of the children.

Everyone was occupied—whether alone, in pairs, or in small groups. The age range was broad. The children wore very casual clothes—clothes they could get dirty without fear of a scolding. There was a busy hum, but it was quiet enough to converse easily. At times, a child brought a product to show the teacher, and in return she would offer words of encouragement and a challenge.

We stepped outside for a while so she could speak freely about the children. I noticed that she didn't put anyone in charge, in fact she didn't say a thing before we left. Anyone who needed her came and sought her out, then returned to the classroom. When we rejoined the group, the level of activity was unchanged, the children still focused on their tasks.

In this classroom, the children had adapted to parameters the adults had given them, and they were learning and progressing commensurate with their individual capacities. Some may have been slow—my daughter was one such, almost a non-reader at the end of first grade—while others flew ahead. I met a first-grader who was doing fifth-grade mathematics. He, too, was classed as a non-reader, but he had learned to decode the symbols and words he needed to understand math.

In this classroom, the children adapted so well, the teacher had to adjust the environment continually just to keep ahead of them.

Vignette 3: Open Classroom Magnet School

As a consultant, I witnessed the developmental stages of a magnet school for fifth- and sixth-grade children in the Pittsburgh public school system.

Children were accepted on a random basis from a city-wide pool of applicants. The only stipulation was that the children had to get to school via public transportation, and a free bus pass was provided.

It took a whole semester for the teachers and students to make the transition. Coming from a background where discipline centers on the teacher, at first no one knew quite how to handle a classroom where children assumed responsibility for their own behavior. The children, responding to their unaccustomed freedom, would go off and hide, hanging out in the bathrooms, seeking refuge in alcoves. When you asked what they were hiding from, they could not tell you.

But it had all turned around by January. The children had identified projects in which they had strong personal commitments. They were given more and more freedom, which they learned to use in a disciplined and problem-solving manner.

For example, the students as a group decided to create their own newspaper and publish the variety of writing they were producing so prolifically. In time, the student editors of the paper became selective, rejecting some submissions. The result? The students whose work was excluded got together and published an alternative paper.

This was the environment in which Justin, whom I mentioned in the previous chapter, blossomed from a non-learner to a non-stop achiever. The degree of initiative these students displayed, the quality of the work they produced, and the rate of their progress was a testament to their increasing self-discipline.

Vignette 4: A First-Grade Math Class

The date is 1990, and the setting is an inner-city parochial school in Pittsburgh. We are visiting a first-grade class in which the children are being taught to think like mathematicians.

The class is divided into teams. The teacher introduces the problem which, more than likely, will take each team three or four days to solve. During their orientation, the teams are encouraged to find alternate solutions to the problem. (Remember back in our own school days when there was only one right answer?) The teams are permitted to move freely about the school, to interview other students, to pursue any reasonable action as they collect the information they need to solve the problem. On the last day, representatives from each team present their findings and discuss the reasoning that led to their approach.

It's a very exciting math class. The kids are so intrigued by their subject, they're prepared to devote all their energy to it.

And then they move on to second grade.

Their new teacher hands out traditional math problems and begins to teach a traditional math lesson. The children revolt. The more articulate ones speak out: They're not children, they're mathematicians. They want to be treated as thinking people.

Although children may adapt complacently to a new learning environment, once they have had a chance to get the bit in their teeth, you had better be prepared to let them run—and at times, to stand aside and let a better mind surpass your own.

Summary

It should be clear from these vignettes that children can adapt to almost any environment we adults design. It is my belief that when schools are failing children it is not the children who are at fault. It is the system and its effect on the teacher that needs to be changed. We have more effective models. It is time that we put them to use.

What Children Bring with Them When They Enter School

Children accomplish a tremendous amount of natural learning between birth and age six. And they do this learning largely on their own. In his book *The Magical Child*, Joseph Chilton Pearce documents the extent of this learning which we as parents, watching our babies grow day by day into school-age children, can easily miss. We indulge a blind faith that our children will learn to speak, and they do, with very little help from us. We encourage them to take their first steps, but they learn to walk pretty much on their own, and we rue the day they can run faster than we. All of this takes place supported only by our respectful faith that they will naturally learn these basics.

Throughout infancy, children are afforded a great deal of respect and encouragement as free-spirited inquirers learning how to speak, walk, and interact with adults and other children. They enter school with enthusiasm and excitement, expecting the same degree of respect.

Instead, they encounter a formal classroom setting that hasn't varied in its basic structure for 150 years. We treat the learning process as we do the manufacture of a machine on a production line: input child, age six. Add reading, math, science, social studies, and output child twelve years later. What happened to that happy, creative learner who entered school with a natural hunger to explore? A few lucky ones make it through the system with their creativity more or less intact—though there's no telling how they might have flourished in a more progressive setting. But many are numbed by the process. These will make good production line workers, but unfortunately, we have automated our production lines. What's left for them? And what's left for the ones who simply don't make it through the system?

Politicians look at the results of standardized tests and lament because children of other cultures surpass our children's scores. So they attempt to produce a world-class student by turning up the heat. Let's develop stricter assessment parameters for teachers. Let's put more pressure on the systems. Let's try for total quality management, and we will produce a student who is competitive in the world markets.

Children entering the classroom for the first time are human beings. Assuming that they come from reasonably functional families, they probably have all of their learning faculties in good order. What can we do to optimize the environment into which we place our children? How can we help them expand and build upon the skills and learning styles they have so cleverly mastered in their first six years of life?

We need to throw out our production line approach to education and make way for a new approach, one that respects the defining quality of humanity in our children. Therefore, we must look at what it means to be human. What is it that distinguishes us from animals?

I recently encountered a young couple who showed me, with considerable pride, the accomplishments displayed by their nine-month-old daughter. She could hold up one finger upon being asked her age, wave goodbye, and give grandma a kiss on command. As they were leaving, I asked how they communicated all this to a preverbal child. They said it was easy; they simply trained her as they did their Labrador retriever, with signs, repeated commands, and treats to reward the targeted behavior. I asked if they could also get their child to roll over on command. They were sure they could.

Today's system of classroom learning utterly fails to account for the essential humanity of our children. We know how to condition our children as we would condition animals. What we need to discover is how to respect our children as humans entering the learning environment.

Let me stress that it's not the teachers who are at fault. Of everyone involved in the school system today, teachers are the most humane in their work with children. It is the system itself that is at fault as it dictates how teachers must perform their job. And it is our society, our politicians, and our boards of education that perpetuate the system.

This leaves parents as the principal agents of change. The parents are the ones who must fight city hall on behalf of their children.

Faith in our children's ability to learn and sort things out for themselves will distinguish the twenty-first century school. Exciting new developments crop up in education every day, and many of these developments will help to transform our schools tomorrow. But we need to begin by building on the natural learning skills of the child first entering school. We need to begin by examining what distinguishes the children of human beings. Are we attending to these human dimensions as we plan the educational environment to which we commit our children for their learning years?

When we start to address these questions, we will initiate the evolution of our schools into productive learning environments rich in stimulating resources—where the teacher functions as mediator and guide in a child-centered, individualized learning program.

Chapter 3
Our Educational Heritage

Leslie Hart's illuminating and powerful essay on the precursors of our current predicament appears here courtesy of Wayne Jennings, editor of *The Brain Based Education Networker.*

Classrooms Are Killing Learning:
A History of the Graded Classroom
Leslie A. Hart

Scene: A local school.
Time: Early morning on a bright spring weekday.

Enter teachers, specialists, and principal, none too cheerfully, to operate an educational system that cannot be operated, that is 150 years old and 100 years out of date, and that daily frustrates everybody in it—students, teachers, and administrators.

It's hard to find anybody who's happy with this effort. Public education absorbs more than half the revenues generated by local and state taxes. As enrollments decline, it costs more and more to serve fewer and fewer, and the results keep sliding down—in learning, achievement, discipline, and morale. Though the scene I've described takes place in an elementary school, there are already problems of drug abuse, alcohol use, and violence.

One might suppose then, that many of those who work inside the schools are giving serious thought to change—to alternative systems—if only to preserve their jobs or create a workplace that is not drenched with failure, confrontation, and searing public criticism. Sad to say, in this school, and tens of thousands like it, in urban, suburban, and rural communities across the land, only the most trivial changes win any consideration. Change in these schools is, in the classic phrase, like rearranging the deck chairs on the Titanic. Many school people are counting the years to retirement or some other escape, or ticking off the weeks to the temporary Nirvana of summer vacation; others are reading the "help wanted" ads every morning.

The core cause of these difficulties has, for the most part, been ignored: the classroom, the Curse of Horace Mann. My educational travels have given me the opportunity to ask many dozens of audiences for one good reason why we should continue to use the graded classroom that Horace Mann, in his praiseworthy drive to give the nation publicly supported common schools, foisted upon us well over a century ago. The first reasonable answer has yet to come my way. In fact, the question has met with puzzlement, incredulity, and even outrage. It seems that many teachers cannot conceive of any other plan for the organization of schools and read into my query a threat to their employment. Administrators seem to take the question less personally, and less seriously, as though I had asked why a school needed lighting or plumbing or floors. Yet I have been in Montessori schools which have functioned for decades without a vestige of a classroom. And I have spent many hours in truly "open" schools where, despite the presence of the original classroom walls, there is hardly a trace of classroom groupings or activities. In London, England I have watched children in a school where few of the rooms had four walls, and the outside areas could be used at will whenever weather permitted.

In our own country—until the invention and dispersion of that triumph of modern civilization, the yellow school bus—the "factory" school was by no means universal. In 1870, the reported 142,000 schools in this country had about 220,000 teachers, or roughly 1.5 each on the average, which means that the great majority of schools were the one-room type. Almost all of them were the "practical" American kind, not relics of the classics-oriented memorize-and-recite European schools. Even as classroom-style schools multiplied in cities, most children who went to school attended one-roomers where, because of total mixed ages and irregular attendance, there was hardly a trace of classroom operation. Though their resources were rock-bottom minimal, and their teachers, usually female, were largely untrained, these schools functioned surprisingly well into our present century. To doubt that there are other ways of organizing schools, or that new ways can be devised, is to ignore how tens of millions of students were educated in the past—at least as successfully as they are today.

Horace Mann's Objectives

I define a classroom as a fixed group of students, selected largely by age, who are confined for most of their school time to a single room, normally for a school year, in the charge of and instructed by a single teacher. At secondary levels, the principle does not change, but applies by subject. Usually, classrooms are "graded," again dominantly by age. In physical terms, the room characteristically is square, bare, and thick-walled, intended to isolate its group from the rest of the school. Classroom schools blatantly reflect the factory plan: children, the raw material, are to be batch processed room by room until they are either stamped "educated" or tossed out on the scrap heap.

Educational history can be murky, but Mann's dominant role in popularizing this type of school stands clear. In Prussia he found a system as a starting point, then modified it to meet his need for a cheap system that could be "sold" to a dubious and stingy public. Graded classrooms permitted hiring widows and unmarried women who needed to know only enough to handle one grade at salaries of half or less what males would demand. The classes, once set up, could be greatly expanded to cope with a rising population at almost no added expense. And the whole enterprise could be run like a factory, with female teachers as hands, male principals as foremen, and superintendents as managers. Ironically, Mann, who was ahead of his time in his regard for women, built crude male chauvinism into the very fabric of the schools. Even today, neither teachers nor their organizations seem to realize this point; they complain about everything but the system that makes them the scapegoats.

An intelligent, dedicated, political, and influential person, Mann saw the common school as the answer to most problems, from ignorance and drunkenness to elitism and poor citizenship. (He predicted nine-tenths of all crime would vanish when schools spread.) But as a lawyer with little knowledge of children or education, he assumed—and his intellectual friends agreed—that teaching would automatically produce learning. Though he realized that children differed, he did not foresee how the increasing rigidity of classroom schools would demand that students be alike, and progress at the same rate.

Because it was cheap and manageable, Mann's system took hold rapidly in the more populated areas. Unfortunately, it never really worked for a single day—in the sense of producing learning reliably—and soon turned instead to stressing order, morality, conformity, and molding those behaviors most suitable to producing a docile industrial labor force.

On the learning front, the carnage staggered the mind: only a trickle of students survived "failures" and drop-out to reach the higher grades. The system had hardly been launched when it became clear that teaching did not produce learning, that students were not alike, and that they did not progress uniformly as a factory system required. Innumerable corrective "plans" were put forward. Some helped, but not nearly enough. Those who controlled the schools soon no longer worried about learning failures; it was easy and acceptable to blame students, their families, their ethnic background, or their poverty.

It appeared that the common school was not for the common, although it gave everyone opportunity—opportunity to fail. To this day, those who profess to speak for "minorities" (who cumulatively usually add up to a majority) waste funds and energy on determining which classroom these children shall be confined to, paying almost no heed to the classroom as a device that virtually guarantees disadvantage, discrimination, and destruction for the poor or "different," wherever the bus may stop.

The early class-and-grade schools that sprung from Mann's rousing efforts operated for as few as twelve weeks a year, for perhaps six grades. But steadily the load put upon this already unworkable system was increased in weeks per year and years of sequence, and the screws were turned tighter by enforced compulsory attendance and, finally, by the drying up of jobs for youngsters—jobs that had for a full century prevented the "scrap heap" from looming larger than the school.

Perhaps history will decide that it was educators' inability to stop the introduction of the National Assessment of Education Progress (NAEP) that marked the beginning of the end of public school classrooms. Once attention was turned to what students had actually learned, the scandal was public. (NAEP, of course, does not try to measure what is learned in school, but only what students can answer.) Other studies of learning achieved became feasible, producing findings ranging from the discouraging to the horrifying. Forced to act by revelations that many high school graduates could not read their diplomas, that the armed forces had to reject huge numbers of applicants, that employers were appalled by the unreadiness of new employees for even the simplest tasks, legislatures in most states have mandated minimal learning outcomes.

In short, the mission of the schools has changed from custody and keeping some degree of order to producing learning by all students. If my observations do not mislead me, few teachers and not many principals and other administrators have yet fully grasped this fundamental change. Some who have, realize they don't have the faintest idea of how to bring about more and better learning. They become paralyzed, not knowing which way to turn. They rearrange the deck chairs, but they don't look for learning solutions.

We simply must face the fact that conventional "teacher-driven" classrooms cannot possibly produce the reliable learning we must attain if schools are to survive. The results of many studies confirm that the 145-year-old system we are still trying to use after 145 years of failure must be scrapped and replaced. Small improvements, even if attainable, will not stave off the collapse.

(*The Brain Based Education Networker*
[Fall 1992]: pp. 2–3, 6)

Part 2
A Rule-Based Philosophy of Education

Chapter 4
The social-cultural environment, a limited democracy where students learn to harmoniously interact, hour by hour, day by day, becomes the community where self-initiated learning flourishes

Chapters 5, 6, 7, 8
The new basic skills of focused behavior, self-initiation, thinking, and creativeness, the four rules of lifelong learning, are presented with some new insights to support the tenet that these are the key elements of child empowerment

Chapter 4
Life-Coping Skills/School as Community

Many educators, with industry hard on their heels, are beginning to study distinct aspects of behavior that successful people have in common. They have found that well-developed social skills seem to be of primary importance in distinguishing the successful from the merely average.

Norman Zuckerman, managing editor of the *New York Post* when President Clinton first took office, described the president on the evening of his inauguration as a man with "great political skill and great human skills." As parents, we would be pleased as punch if some notable person said that of our children. But our present form of education does little to equip our youth with human skills.

Traditional education focuses only on fact-based knowledge, on memorizing information and parroting it back. We have sophisticated educational tools and concepts in our present educational system, such as computer-assisted learning, thinking skills, integrated learning, and hands-on science, yet the development of all the *social* qualities which we so admire in successful people is left entirely to chance. Children are boxed up in classrooms with teachers who are afraid to let them express themselves for fear they will get out of hand. Such dimensions as self-initiation, good social skills, and self-expression—all of the skills that seem to define successful adults—are notably absent in the traditional curriculum. And yet, at the end of their formal educational experience, we are surprised that our graduates do not immediately succeed in their new jobs.

If you took a hard look at successful life-coping skills, and then determined what training might result in such skills, early childhood education would take on an entirely different character. A well-honed, compassionate human being does not simply happen, but is crafted over time; yet we neglect the crafting process. Parents are too busy earning a living, teachers are overburdened with administrative tasks, and the other institutions in our society don't get enough of the child's time to have any influence. Except for a very few exceptional programs, television, which gets the lion's share of our children's attention, only degrades human development.

What Makes Us Human?

When I began searching through diverse literature to discover those qualities that distinguish man from lesser beings, I had already concluded that one of the defining characteristics of the O/PE movement was that children were treated as human beings and were gently encouraged in developing human qualities. I wanted to establish that there is more to educating youth than fact-based knowledge.

In my readings, I identified many characteristics that distinguish man from animals. Leakey suggested six essential qualities: consciousness, compassion, morality, language, creativity, and culture. Fromm described five: awareness of self, imagination, reason, inner strength, and self-reliance. May identified just one, freedom, and equated it with human dignity. To this list, I considered adding self-initiation and effort, pride in craftsmanship, and interpersonal behavior.

These were all thought-provoking concepts, but so far I sensed no unifying force. I did not know exactly what I was seeking: something to convince structuralists (which one British professor called the force in England that was causing their education system to follow America's cry for more of the basics) that we must pay more attention to shaping the human character of our youth.

I finally found my answer in Leakey's *Origins Reconsidered*. It might not change the thinking of millions of Americans, but for me it was a great *aha*, a great insight. Discussing how the brain has evolved through the ages, Leakey noted that the chimpanzee's brain is far larger than necessary for food-gathering, reproduction, and general survival. Searching to explain this incongruity, anthropologists concluded that the additional brain capacity enabled individual chimps to survive within a complex social structure. This is stated more fully in the following passage, condensed from Leakey's book:

The cognitive skills displayed by higher primates in the laboratory seem to outstrip by far the practical demands of their natural worlds. Has natural selection been profligate in making them smarter than they really need to be?

A few years ago, Cambridge University psychologist Nicholas Humphrey visited Kenya, where we talked about his ideas. What, I wanted to know, did these observations have to do with the evolution of the human mind? "The same things you can say about the daily lives of gorillas—that the world of practical affairs seems to be very demanding intellectually—you can say about humans," he replied. "Studies on hunter-gatherer societies show that the demands of their daily lives are not great. Hunting techniques do not greatly outstrip those of other social carnivores. And gathering strategies are of the same order as you might find in, say, chimpanzees or baboons."

I acknowledged this and wondered what it was in evolutionary history that enabled the human brain to create a Mozart symphony or Einstein's theory of relativity. *"The answer,"* said Nick, *"is social life. Primates lead complex social lives. That is what makes them—and has made us—so intelligent."* [italics mine] I must admit to having been pretty skeptical about Nick's suggestion during that trip. . . . The notion that the exigencies of social interaction . . . may have been responsible for honing human intellect seemed somehow insubstantial. Perhaps it is because the social nexus is so natural a part of human existence that it becomes, in a way, invisible to our thought. A decade of research on nonhuman primates has, however, had the effect of making the social nexus not only visible but also sharply focused. Nick's hypothesis now looks very powerful indeed. (Pp. 284–285)

How have we missed this point in the education of human children? Aren't effective social skills the very skills that differentiate successful adults from the unsuccessful? From this passage, I concluded that social, life-coping skills are far more important than most academic subjects that students currently spend untold hours mastering.

The realm of social skills is made up of behaviors that are not academic: interpersonal relations, responsibility, trustworthiness, creativity and self-reliance. Consider for a moment the skills we so admire in successful adults—people who really shine as they walk through their daily routine:

- They are articulate—they have a good command of language and can express themselves well.

- They are self-confident.

- They are popular, frequently taking on leadership roles.

- They are reliable and dependable.

- They have a positive attitude toward life.

- Their cup of resources is overflowing—they approach life with a giving perspective.

- They have good thinking skills.

- They are reasonable and open-minded, not biased.

- They are expert at negotiation.

- They are good sports, who win with modesty and accept defeat with grace.

These are people who dance well with life, unselfishly, with respect and compassion for others.

Social Skills Are Learned through Experience

I suspect that those attributes that make President Clinton a man with great human skills were learned outside the classroom. We develop much of our social and life-coping skill from observing others who are older and more experienced than we are. Highly-controlled classrooms misshape our children by limiting their opportunities for social observation.

Curricula exist that can teach children these skills, but they lack the impact that results when children live by these principles each day. The problem is not our methods so much as the time we allow for practice. Children learn to apply human education only by living these concepts, and this is an area in which current education fails.

The social skills we learned in school came from informal encounters with our peers, in the hallways and lunchrooms, traveling to and from school, and participating in after-school activities. Since the school did not foster these encounters, shy kids had no opportunity to learn to express themselves in safe settings, while bullies acted out aggressive, attention-getting behavior and never learned acceptable alternatives. And yet these informal encounters, which the schools deemed so unimportant, may make all the difference in determining who will be a successful person and who will not.

Over the next few days, try asking yourself how many of the skills you use came from academic learning and how many are the result of life experience. While the knowledge and training that allow you to practice your profession stem mostly from academics, the manner in which you practice—the way that you communicate, negotiate, and show compassion in your daily life—comes almost exclusively from experience.

Reflect for a moment about social skills exhibited by chimpanzees. How are they learned? They're certainly not taught. Some part may be instinctual, but much more is learned through observation, play, trial and error: *What can I get away with?* A relevant question for humans as well as chimps.

Both children and chimps need an environment in which to practice interpersonal skills, to test the limits and to be challenged when they go too far. These skills can only be perfected in a realistic setting, where teachers take on a key role as arbitrators, giving students labels for behavior and helping them think through the ramifications of their acts.

By closely attending to our children as they develop their human qualities, we will foster graduates whose inner strength, self-reliance, and self-awareness far exceed that of traditional school graduates. The key to all of this is the development of a school community where the culture focuses on developing and honoring our unique attributes as human beings.

As Leakey says, "I believe that the qualities of humanness—consciousness, compassion, morality, language—arose gradually in our history, products of the evolutionary process that shaped our species. These qualities are, of course, most appropriate in the interactions among individual humans; they are the threads that hold social fabric together." (Ibid., p. 358)

An Intense Caring Community

"The threads that hold social fabric together" may be the same threads that underlie the culture of the school based on self-initiated learning. Such a learning environment teaches academic skills while including the broadest array of life-coping skills.

The fully-functional O/PE environment is a micro-model of a caring community: an extended family in which children, practicing good social skills on a daily basis, are removed of their sharp edges and honed to a high degree of habitual and compassionate behavior. Children learn to cooperate with each other on projects of mutual interest. Older students help the younger ones learn to share resources and work out their differences. The school begins to fill a void in the lives of many children who, living in single-parent or two-earner households, are left without adult guidance for a good part of the day. The variety of people in this community becomes a resource in itself. When children are given a safe place to practice self-expression and try out ideas, shyness gives way to self-confidence. All are encouraged to find their own ways to excel.

The teacher and the students create this democratic micro-culture together. Over time, each student learns to participate as a fully-functioning member of the community. Working through their lessons in this setting, students learn a host of social skills by interacting with others undertaking similar projects. When children are encouraged to talk freely with each other in a setting modeled after the real world, life-coping skills are a natural by-product of the experience. Valued relationships exist between children of all ages. Many bonds established in the open classroom are life long.

When the Irwin Avenue School has an open house for prospective students, graduates come to talk about their elementary school experiences. They are very articulate, think well on their feet, address the audience with poise, respond intelligently to questions, and seem to feel very good about themselves without appearing smug. They have gone on to become popular kids in high school, often attaining leadership roles in school government and other activities. And they built the confidence to do this simply by living and practicing good social, life-coping skills every day in their earlier education. It is through these graduates that the school sells itself to doubting parents.

To develop social skills, children must come to have faith in themselves, their beliefs, their creative capacities, and their compassion for others. A reductionist would attempt to teach each of these variables singly, leaving the child to combine them somehow into interrelated wholes. But leading scientists are walking away from the reductionist viewpoint, studying life, nature, matter, and the universe in terms of their overall interrelatedness.

In this environment, where sound ethical values are modeled on a daily basis, each child can fully develop all of those qualities that characterize "great human skills."

The School Culture as a Learning Environment

Three factors provide the basis for a learning environment that will nurture the hungry mind. They are:

- The size of the school, which cannot exceed 250 children

- The governance of the school, a limited democracy run by the students and faculty

- The moral fabric of the school, celebrating in every way possible the humanity of students and teachers

The objective is to create a community in which it is safe for students to explore what it means to be a human being. A safe place to learn, where others actively try to understand you, where there is little threat or coercion, where the lines of communication remain open in all directions. The caring community provides a place for debates and disagreements, with sufficient controls to ensure that they don't get out of hand. A place where students learn about compromise and tolerance. A place where these skills can be practiced as they naturally evolve, moment to moment, day to day.

What constitutes a true learning community?

I would suggest these prerequisites: authentic human teacher guides, empathic relationships; a great deal of freedom, respect for everyone, especially students; faith in children's ability to learn and explore; continuous communication and continuous inquiry; social interactive skills and an emphasis on developing our humanity.

Built into this learning environment is an opportunity to develop and explore all forms of relationships. After all, life is really about relationships. We live fully when we relate well to the people around us. In the end, academic learning is only a small piece of the pie we call life.

The Learning Environment

Recent research findings suggest that children learn best when the school population is kept relatively small. The closeness of such a setting enhances learning. Everyone knows everyone else. Teachers and administrators can learn the name of every child in the school. Freedom, trust and respect are key attributes that dominate interaction. Hall passes are unnecessary; students come and go as their needs dictate.

I know of one such school where students go to lunch whenever they choose. It's a cherished privilege which also serves as a behavioral control: the privilege can be revoked. By respecting this, students can decide whom they wish to have lunch with, as adults do, and they do this responsibly and without disruption. They learn what it means to be trusted, and they learn to feel better about themselves.

This fosters a strong learning culture, in which not only the teacher's expectations are very high, but the students also set high standards for themselves. End products become prized examples of each student's best work. At the Vermont-based Prospect School, mentioned in an earlier chapter, the students' portfolios have been so consistently impressive that scholars have micro-filmed them for extended study.

The self-initiated learning model recognizes children as more than empty vessels to be filled, placing emphasis instead on the multitude of accomplishments and the keenness of mind the child brings upon entering school.

Freedom and Discipline

Freedom abounds in these schools. Children assert their freedom to choose when they select an area on which to focus their efforts. By accepting their choices, we as adults demonstrate our respect for each child. Respect forms the foundation of trust, which is essential to building a sound student-teacher relationship.

When we deny students the freedom to choose, we enslave them. And thus begins the student's battle to gain freedom. This antagonistic relationship is counterproductive to learning and to self-realization. The school dropout is seeking human dignity through freedom. That is why City-As-School is so successful. An alternative work-study program offered through the National Diffusion Network, City-As-School allows students sufficient freedom to develop a sense of human dignity while still obtaining an education.

In *Freedom and Destiny*, Rollo May asserts that freedom is essential to human dignity: "Powerlessness, we know, is tantamount to slavery. It is a truism that, if people are to have freedom, they must have the equivalent personal power in the form of autonomy and responsibility." (P. 10) As the anthropologist

Bronislaw Malinowski puts it, "Freedom is the *possibility* of 'self-realization' based on personal choice, on free contract and spontaneous endeavor, or individual initiative." (Ibid., p. 10) The teacher/guide's role is to help children understand how to use their freedom creatively.

But how do we sell parents on the idea of allowing children freedom? Parents equate freedom of choice with the acting-out behavior that comes about when children are suddenly set free.

There are numerous ways order is maintained in the self-initiated learning environment while still giving the student the sense of total freedom. The primary controller of behavior is the students themselves, not because they are practicing restraint, but simply because they are fully engaged in projects or activities they have undertaken, whether it be an inquiry into a question raised, or an engaging hour of chess, or an hour of work on a creative project, or an in-depth discussion as a member of a group undertaking.

When students are encouraged to recognize their freedom as a privilege, rather than a right, they place their own restraints on behavior and become more sensitive to thoughtless acts. After all, isn't this how our society is structured? People have freedom to do as they wish, as long as what they do is within the prescribed limits, the laws of the state. If one exceeds these limits, then one loses a privilege, as drunken drivers lose their licenses.

The same holds true in progressive schools. The limits are precisely defined, and all present have a say in establishing the laws by which they live.

In this micro-society, there emerges over time a collection of rules that have been developed by the students and teacher through a limited democracy. As incidents occur, they are brought up in discussion at class meetings. Acceptable patterns of behavior are agreed upon and noted in the class rules of behavior. Unacceptable behaviors are discussed, and acceptable alternatives are proposed by both the offenders and their classmates. This important process not only models democratic principles at work, it also causes students to consider the consequences of their behavior.

Rules such as: I will not disturb others who are actively engaged in studies; I will consider others' feelings; I will avoid disturbing noises, destruction of property, personal squabbles, and messiness are typical of those developed by students and teachers.

The freedom students gain is an enabling, energizing force that helps them focus self-initiating skills, practice effective interpersonal relationships, and hone thinking skills. Freedom is an extremely important component of the child's developing sense of human dignity. When freedom is properly orchestrated by the teacher, it becomes the component that underlies the child's emerging love of school and learning. Reflect once again upon what Rollo May has to say about the importance of freedom in our lives: "Freedom is essential to human dignity." (Ibid., p. 9)

What Makes a Community?

All of this alone does not make a community. These are all components of a very complex system of learning. I have extracted these pieces to show you a portion of the puzzle, but they do not yet add up to a complete picture.

A community emerges when teachers discover the richness of working with children in the self-initiated learning environment. This experience enhances the lives of teachers as well as students, and they share the richness with their colleagues—and then the whole close-knit community comes alive. Parents become an integral part of this community through the enthusiasm of their children, through volunteer time in the classroom, through conferences with their children's teachers. This, in turn, begins to tie families together as they meet and share their concerns and their enthusiasm.

There is enormous potential for revitalization of the entire community served by the school. This builds into a whole new culture, in which children love school; it is no longer students against teachers, us against them.

We celebrate our humanity with certain standards by which we live, and students learn to emulate these standards in the proper setting. Rather than elaborating on each of the human attributes here, I wish simply to point out that we need to be aware of these uniquely human traits and do our best to ensure their full development in our children. It should be part of our daily list of things to do: *I will be compassionate with my fellow beings, be moral in my decisions and relationships, be open to all points of view, and be creative. Be self-reliant and call on my inner strength to get over the hurdles, both large and small.*

Keep this framework in mind as you go about your daily life. Make a mental note whenever human skills arise, either in your life or your child's. You will begin to appreciate how your children can only realize their full potential if they develop these essential skills.

Chapter 5
Long-Term Attending Skills

Rule 1: Support the establishment of long-term attending skills in young children.

The ability to focus on a task for an extended period is crucial to any child's development. This skill will be a valuable asset, not only during the school years, but throughout the child's life. By providing guidance and modeling, teachers and older students help the child choose a task and learn to stick with it.

I learned to do long division very quickly, back in the fourth grade. I immediately understood how the algorithm worked, and my teacher sent me home with a note to my parents, complimenting me on my accomplishment. That was such a good reinforcer, I remember it to this day. But in spite of it, I soon grew impossibly bored as the teacher went over and over and over the process for slower classmates. I did not remain challenged, so my mind began to wander. Eventually I lost my earlier sense of focus, thereby losing out on a prime opportunity to develop long-term attending skills.

To succeed in any challenging endeavor, we need a well-developed ability to focus our attention. Biologists and architects, composers and authors, in fact anyone who undertakes a complex task must remain focused on it for an extended time. Today's computer programmers and researchers studying artificial intelligence work long hours, day after day, to create, test and refine their work. Those who successfully tackle larger mysteries must wrestle with a single problem for years, whether their object is to develop vertical flight, like Sikorski, or a theoretical basis for space and time, like Einstein, or a symphonic masterpiece, like Mozart.

But where and when in traditional school settings are students given the opportunity to commit long periods to a serious inquiry? Anyone can come up with a few isolated instances where a bright child displayed highly-focused behavior, but they are the exceptions rather than the rule.

These are extremely important habits of mind that must be established early in life, then encouraged and sustained throughout the school career. Once firmly ingrained, they will become a valuable resource which today's children will call upon as adults in order to solve life's complex problems. And the open/progressive education movement has proven that the best time to begin this training is when the child first enters school.

With no formal coaching, children focus on exploring their environment almost from birth. Preschoolers can pursue games of imagination for hours on end. In her book *I Learn from Children,*

Caroline Pratt describes how well young children remain focused on building blocks and dramatic play. The process is even more effective in multiple-age classrooms, where younger children join older ones in projects that last for hours or even days.

When I visited the Irwin Avenue School, one teacher described her success in shaping a first-grader's long-term attending skills. Initially, whenever this child faced a problem of some complexity, she would try to opt out by lamenting over its difficulty and pleading with the teacher or other students for help. She even threw temper tantrums.

On the day of my visit, this same child was singled out by her teacher for special recognition during family meeting time. She and a friend had just completed a sixty-piece puzzle. Although she had approached the task with her usual litany of laments, once she focused her attention she forgot to complain, and ultimately succeeded.

She interrupted us while I was talking with her teacher, wanting a newly-finished page in her math workbook checked off. By learning to focus, she now easily accomplished a task which she would previously have been reluctant even to begin. It has taken her teacher a year to shape this behavior, which the child will further refine into a lifelong asset of immense value.

In the K–3 (kindergarten through third grade) class that I visited, a whole culture has grown up around chess. Children who have become skilled in the game are sought out by others who wish to refine their own skills. Recognizing the value of this focused behavior, the school has begun to support it. A chess teacher visits the class each week and helps students at all levels develop their proficiency. This focused behavior enhances thinking skills and helps to exercise the child's mind.

Ideally, such skills are not developed in isolation, but in the diversity that exists in an open/progressive education classroom. This situation brings together older children, who can provide a model and leadership, with younger ones, who seek them out for learning opportunities. Equally important, the children are expanding their social interaction skills every day. The teachers need only assist with problems and occasionally prod the learners to explore other points of view.

Consider for a moment the type of program we inflict on Headstart children, or for that matter traditional kindergarten students. They work on tasks built around the premise that their attention span is no more than fifteen or twenty minutes. In a classroom of twenty-five to thirty children who are just starting school, the teacher has to keep up the pace: twenty minutes of this and twenty minutes of that. Never does the child have an opportunity to become focused. Never does the child have an opportunity to begin developing any semblance of long-term attending skills.

In contrast, an open/progressive education classroom brings together children at three grade levels and all stages of focused behavior development. This fosters acquisition of skills through intense interaction. Now the kindergarten children have models to follow. Now the teacher is in a better position to help these children find something on which to focus. Anything will do. A sixty-piece puzzle provided a more than adequate challenge for a first-grader. Get the focused behavior established first. After children start to show a tendency toward long-term attending skills, they are better prepared to begin academic study.

Time on Task

Research studies of students in traditional classroom settings have found a distinct relationship between the time students spend focused on a task and their level of achievement. These findings clearly support the argument for highly-focused behavior. But time spent on task represents only one aspect of long-term attending skills. What these studies do not address are differences in student motivation, learning retention, and the consequent degree of efficiency in the learning process.

In traditional schools, students who study hard do well on tests. But such tests tell us only how well the students have memorized the material. These short-term measures of achievement do not tell us how well they actually *understand* the material, how long they will retain it, or whether they can apply it in real-life settings.

In contrast, when students develop long-term attending skills, they acquire a habitual behavior that helps them focus effectively on almost anything that interests them—or, for that matter, any problem they confront. Thus, the girl who developed the persistence and patience to put together a sixty-piece puzzle was also able to complete her daily math assignment without a whimper.

In that same school, three girls in the fourth- and fifth-grade class were working to decipher the concept of simple calculations involving fractions and whole numbers. Using disks and parts of disks as manipulatives, they set out together to understand the process more fully. Clearly they had developed good focusing habits, as they stayed with the task for an hour or more. Occasionally, the teacher would stop by to add new insights into their problem-solving. Suddenly, there were exclamations of delight as symbolic operations became clear through the manipulatives. The group immediately launched into an exploration of larger numbers and more complex operations.

There was no external force coercing them to stay on task. No one said, "You can't leave until you solve the problem." In fact, other students pestered them to get on with it so that they, too, could use the materials at that learning station. These intruders were chased away.

These three girls saw the simple pursuit of new concepts as an engaging hour. Other children may require different motivators, which can often be found in open/progressive education classrooms. Caroline Pratt relates an example in which social pressure provided motivation: At one point in the evolution of the City and Country School, the second-grade class was responsible for running the school store. "One little girl was so slow in making out sales slips that she held up the customers until they became critical, not to say abusive. Her small partners in business found that she did not know even the simplest of the tables, and they took away her job until she could make good. She learned some of the tables overnight." (*I Learn from Children*, p. 103)

Caroline Pratt recognized the need to establish long-term attending skills as early as the mid-thirties: "Frank as usual had a card made out for shop, made out till 3:30, the longest possible period (one hour and a half), and another for an after school appointment. He is making window boxes for his mother and is insistent on finding time to finish them. In view of the fact that he had been reported as lacking in concentration when he first came into the school a year ago, this tendency to work in long periods interests me particularly." (Ibid., p. 114)

If we wish to empower children with lifelong learning skills, we must start by teaching them how to focus on a problem for an extended time. You can begin to shape this behavior by complimenting a child who is deeply engrossed in something of interest. Allowing the child to remain engaged with this task—even if it presents an inconvenience to the rest of the class or in the home—will provide additional reinforcement, which can be very effective for a child who seems to have difficulty focusing.

However, we should be careful when selecting a focused behavior to reinforce. The activity can't simply be engaging, it must also present an appropriate mental challenge. For example, I would almost never reinforce television viewing, but I might compliment a child for a focused game of checkers, and gradually encourage him to tackle a greater challenge, such as chess. Although these activities are not part of the traditional curriculum, chess playing, like piecing together a complex puzzle, constitutes good mental gymnastics. The more fully a mind is exercised, the more its neural pathways grow.

Learn to show respect for focused minds. If your children are absorbed in some activity, don't push them to come running at your command. Develop a disengaging routine, a five-minute warning to let them know that they must come to dinner or change activities. Help them learn to make note of where they are in a group discussion or a game of chess, so they can pick up again where they left off. With complex projects, such as large block buildings, consider allowing them to continue with their project later, and ask other children to respect the effort that has gone into its construction. Then help celebrate the final product to further reinforce the focused behavior of its creator.

What will all of this focused behavior do for children? It will teach them to engage in any task persistently and patiently, to see it through every nuance, until it has evolved into a well-conceived end product, whether it be a term paper or a novel, a well-rehearsed play or a refined piece of art. You will have given a child a truly valuable lifelong skill!

Chapter 6
Self-Initiated Learning

Rule 2: Support, focus and shape self-initiating behaviors in young children.

Self-initiation is another key to being successful in life, yet traditional schools do not allow this talent to emerge. Nothing is accomplished in the self-initiated learning environment without the student making it happen. This chapter explores various dimensions of self-initiation and the reasons for its inclusion in a school that focuses on empowering the child.

To be good citizens, we must actively participate in the democratic process. Yet today, politicians and reporters lament over poor showing at the polls. To become successful in the new jobs now emerging, we must draw on self-initiated skills. Yet today, business owners complain about the passivity of their new employees. As a country, we admire and pay tribute to the self-starter in our society, yet we do nothing to foster this behavior as our youth proceed through school. With rare exceptions, we inhibit and even punish self-initiated behavior. Instead of encouraging students to explore their own emerging ideas, we insist that they put them aside, work on them only after school, after homework, after chores, after everything else that has been assigned by parents and teachers is out of the way.

What a gross mistake! We are telling our children that their own ideas and interests are of no value. *Listen to the adults. They have all the answers. They will educate you. They know the proper way.* Think of what this does to our children's self-image, to their sense of self-worth, to their thinking skills and the development of self-reliance that they will need in later life.

Rollo May states that "the contemporary existentialists see freedom as the quality most threatened by our modern age, with its assembly-line objectification of human persons." (*Freedom and Destiny*, p. 7) I have already described the connection between freedom and human dignity. Now I propose a similar connection between freedom and self-initiated behavior.

It is our natural state to be inquirers, doers, to be dissatisfied with the status quo, always striving for new horizons. Passiveness is an unnatural state that grows out of our loss of freedom. That loss begins when we enter a restrictive school environment, and more often than not endures later in our equally restrictive jobs.

In the self-initiated learning environment, nothing is accomplished without the student making it happen. The environment is designed this way because self-initiation is a key to being successful in life—yet traditional schools suppress this skill.

Before young students can learn self-initiation, the schools must acknowledge the importance of allowing them the freedom to use it. I cannot overstress the importance of students learning to take responsibility for their own acts. Teachers must trust their students with a degree of responsibility that allows them to find their own focal point in their studies.

We now know that when children are encouraged to undertake projects of their own choosing, they release enormous amounts of energy to pursue those projects. They will explore in greater depth, exhibiting the type of self-discipline that wipes away behavioral problems and contributes to a community of inquiry.

Under this system, old behavioral problems, such as acting out for attention, diminish—and new behavioral problems emerge, giving the teacher a new role. Teachers must help overzealous students learn to settle their differences, to appreciate alternative points of view. A teacher will begin to act more as a coach/parent/therapist than simply a disseminator of information. This role calls for a new sort of teaching skills, encouraging and prodding students to look deeper into their subject and to assess different perspectives.

Shaping Self-Initiated Skills in All Aspects of Life

The concept of shaping behavior to develop certain skills comes directly from behavioral psychology. The trick is to catch children applying their initiative in most any non-destructive manner, and actively reward that behavior. It need not be an academic act. It is equally valid to reward activities representing all aspects of a well-fulfilled life, from painting or woodworking to fitness or computer technology.

The real judgment call is to decide, as self-initiated behavior continues, whether at some point it ceases to act as a positive force. A child who is fascinated with a musical instrument may spend untold hours practicing and refining this skill, perhaps laying the foundation for a lifelong interest, whereas a child who becomes devoted to a computer game might eventually be rechanneled into a more purposeful activity.

Given a classroom in which children are expected to write weekly contracts with their teacher, it is easy for the teacher to guide them to the breadth of activities that will help them develop all facets of their education. Parents may also find it helpful to set goals and develop contracts with their children. By this means, you will know your children are gaining a certain breadth of experience while still fostering that sense of perceived choice among the activities available. Furthermore, contracts help you and your children to define limits. Television viewing, for example, both in time and in program selection, is a freedom that you may decide to limit, whereas reading may be encouraged.

Self-initiated activities should not be limited to developing solitary skills. Learning to relate in small and large groups, both as leader and as participant, is a critical skill that may be self-initiated. A child with an idea that requires multiple participants must know how to invite and engage others in the activity. Practice, practice, practice is the key to developing and honing this skill, and that is the beauty of this system: teachers have their students' attention for 180 days a year.

The graduates of schools employing well-conceived models of self-initiated learning have exemplary motivational skills. They know how to get things done. They have inquiring minds and know how to turn ideas into reality. They have well-developed leadership skills. They can take a topic or idea and pull a group together around it, leading it to completion. As a result, they often become class leaders in upper grades and college.

New Beginnings

The idea of dying only to be born anew is common to many of the world's religions. It figures in our secular ceremonies at the end of each year, when we sing out the old year and celebrate the birth of the new year, which is symbolized as a newborn child. The media further this celebration by heralding the first birth of the new year. So it is proper that we celebrate self-initiated behavior. Let the old, outdated learning models die away, and give breathing room to our children's inborn passion to explore the world. It is appropriate to treat this natural ability with respect and help our children learn to shape it to their advantage.

There is a new day dawning. A new century dawning with incredible challenges. Our outdated forms of schooling must be laid to rest with the dying of the twentieth century. Our children and our countrymen deserve to be treated as humans, and only humans have this wonderful power, to focus, plan, and carry out complex endeavors. Let's become experts at empowering our children to grab the initiative and run with it. It is, after all, a natural state of being. Our present environment of continuing restriction can only lead to passivity—a condition we cannot condone in the twenty-first century.

Remember: Nothing happens unless you make it happen. Only you, as a parent, a teacher, a concerned member of the human community, can enable a child to become self-initiating. Encourage your children to become risk-takers, to venture to the very edge of their knowledge and skills.

Technology and Self-Initiated Study

A Vignette

During the Reagan administration, my daughter became so incensed by the president's denial that acid rain represented an environmental problem that she made it the subject of a science project, and set out to design an ambitious study of the effects of acid rain on rivers and lakes in the northeastern United States.

Motivation was not a problem in this inquiry. Instead, she constantly pressured me to help her open new doors. To complete her research, she needed water samples drawn from a number of sites in New England, as well as closer to our Maryland home, so she drew on my network of contacts with educators to identify students in northeastern schools who would draw samples for her study. She wanted to get accurate pH readings on her samples, and the local community college science department had very sensitive pH meters that would do the trick, so I was pressed to open that door. She needed water samples from the Port Tobacco River, an estuary of the Potomac, so we set off at fixed intervals, in rain or shine, to draw them from specific points that were accessible only by boat.

As a parent, I found it fascinating to discuss her findings, both from her readings and from her research, as it contrasted so with President Reagan's assertions. Her anger and frustration with the government only mirrored my own. Looking back on this vignette from the perspective of self-initiated behavior, it is clear to me that the inquiry itself became self-fulfilling and, to some degree, self-perpetuating. In the future, technology will facilitate student inquiries such as this. It will enable students to delve into findings at the cutting edge of important social issues and other topics of immediate interest. In this process they will be well-served by computer bulletin boards, networks, and e-mail (personal computer-based mailboxes).

If schools had been equipped with the appropriate technology when my daughter conducted her study, and if students were in the habit of using this technology on a daily basis, she would have needed only to announce her objective on a computer bulletin board that was read by her peers. Students with similar interests would have responded to her e-mail, and her research would have been greatly expedited.

The same daughter, now in graduate school at the University of Minnesota, has acquired her own computer and her own e-mail address. It will be some time before large numbers of schools connect to online computer networks, but the trend is in that direction.

My position as a parent is that if you want your child to keep up with the forefront of this information age, you had better be ready to provide support whenever needed. We must push for this technology in our schools, and we must support our children's active pursuit of answers through this means.

Chapter 7
Thinking Skills

Rule 3: Enable students to become fluent in all forms of thinking skills through daily use and practice.

Open/progressive education undoubtedly sparked the current surge of interest in thinking skills, as the honing and refinement of these skills lies at the very heart of such a learning environment. Slowly, traditionalists are coming to recognize what open/progressive educators have known for years—that the only way for thinking skills to flourish is to educate our youth in a free-flowing, controlled democracy.

Self-initiated learning is founded on the development, evolution, and honing of inquiry skills. The shaping and cultivation of children's thinking behavior is essential to the development of lifelong learners. Open/progressive educators have long been aware of the importance of thinking skills. John Dewey and his followers recognized their value in the early part of this century. Caroline Pratt, who founded the City and Country School in 1914, wrote extensively in her book *I Learn from Children* about shaping children's natural inquiry skills to a point where they reflect deeply before they ask questions.

In contrast, traditionalists have only recently begun to explore the concept of thinking skills. They have mounted a massive effort to define all of the dimensions of good thinking skills and to map out a plan to integrate the teaching of these skills in all academic areas. This has led to a proliferation of books on thinking skills, discussing the topic from every point of view imaginable. Having scanned a reasonable sampling of this literature, I admit that this effort has made a significant contribution to both traditional and progressive forms of education. Until recently, it was not easy to find well-considered discussions of how all the dimensions of thinking skills fit into an educational program. Through these efforts, new training programs, guidelines, and materials have been developed to help traditional teachers integrate thinking skills into their curricula.

Although I am not a specialist in thinking skills, I have gleaned sufficient understanding from experts I have encountered and through hours of videotaping children in the classroom to appreciate that the schools of the twenty-first century must focus on honing this skill to its finest edge. I find that I intuitively use many of the thinking skills that are being taught in progressive schools today, but as with many readers of this book, I was never privileged to work with the more precisely defined processes that have been recently developed. These mental models are shortcuts to clear thinking, and the students extensively trained in their use whom I have observed are intellectually miles beyond my contemporaries and myself. Such children will have a lifelong competitive edge over their peers who are not trained in thinking skills.

Now comes the question, can you really teach thinking skills, or must you shape thinking skill behavior as it occurs naturally in children's interactions with one another, in their written exploration of ideas, and in the questions they ask adults? Most open/progressive educators feel that you cannot really teach these skills, you have to label and shape them as they occur naturally.

Optimizing thinking skills requires the following conditions:

- Children must be able to converse freely with each other, to develop an unrestricted flow of ideas.

- Children must feel that the classroom is a safe place for them to exercise freedom of thought.

- All who participate in the learning community must demonstrate respect for each other's ideas, no matter how tenuous.

- The setting must encourage and reward expansive writing, which helps to sharpen thinking.

- There must be a special respect for fleeting thoughts and new ideas.

This is an environment in which children are given a great amount of freedom to initiate their own learning experiences and to continuously exchange ideas. You can hear the children thinking.

The key to shaping children's thinking skills begins by learning how *not* to answer their questions. Rather, the teacher/coach must help the student learn to focus on a problem and define its attributes. Caroline Pratt describes how she began the shaping of her student's inquiry skills at the City and Country School:

> Questions came in a steady stream from some of my children when we first began to go on our trips. But when they got their questions turned back on them—"Why do you think the ferry has two round ends?"—they were silenced for a while. When the questions came again they were different. They were not asked just to get attention, to make conversation, or for the dozen reasons besides that of gaining information. They were sincere and purposeful; the question now became what it should be, the first step in the child's own effort to find the answer for himself.
>
> Whether I knew the answer or not, I rarely supplied it on demand. Most answers thus given are a waste of a child's time, if not the adult's. The answer which the child has found out for himself is the one which has meaning for him, both in the information gained and in the experience of finding it. On our trips we found some answers, and some were put over to the future. Open questions are good things to carry around with one; they sharpen the eye and prod the mind; they give the imagination many a practice spin on the way to finding the answer.
>
> (*I Learn from Children*, pp. 45–46)

This technique of turning questions back on the child rather than giving out answers has been used by Stan Pergoff at the University of Arizona, where his Higher Order Thinking Skills (HOTS) program motivates low-achievers to become engaged in the inquiry process, with the goal of reigniting their enthusiasm for learning. HOTS is a pull-out program: for six weeks, students leave their classrooms for a block of time each day, working in the computer labs to solve given problems on their own or in small teams. Even when their questions are as basic as how to operate the computer, the students are encouraged to discover answers for themselves through exploration. Returning from six weeks in the computer lab, these students are truly enthusiastic about learning, with a new self-confidence in their thinking and questioning skills. The program is so successful that many home-based teachers want to adapt it for all of their students.

Training teachers in this technique is a long and intensive process. It has been argued that teachers must be scripted, but in reality, role-playing in realistic scenarios helps them develop clever ways to respond to students' questions without returning direct answers. Teachers take on an artful role in such a learning environment. They must be sensitive to their students' underlying motivation whenever a question is asked and knowledgeable enough to guide the student in the search for answers. They must be willing to enter this world of inquiry with the child when questions are raised that exceed their knowledge base, guiding the child in undertaking an inquiry that will expand both the adult's and the child's understanding.

Throughout their elementary school years, students will undertake the same range of activities over and over again: first discovering a point of interest, then performing an initial investigation, refining their questions, organizing their thoughts, and finally presenting their conclusions. Students enthusiastically undertake these tasks when they are allowed to select topics of interest to them. Because of their enthusiasm, they do not lack motivation, but instead are driven to seek information to depths beyond their assigned tasks. Because the students are enthusiastic about their inquiries, the teacher does not have to deal with disciplinary problems. Because they are enthusiastic, the children take time to edit and refine their reports to a level far beyond usual grade standards. Consider how much practice these children acquire in refined language usage by continually repeating this process, and you will come to appreciate the degree to which this form of education exceeds the parameters of traditional curricula. We are defining an educational experience that enables students to develop their potential to the cutting edge.

The classroom climate here is the reverse of what we see in traditional education, where students do as little as possible to get by. In this new setting the students frequently work in teams on projects, with all members equally pulling their own weight. The classroom mode is quality input and work.

Roger von Oech describes this process of inquiry in colorful terms in his book *A Kick in the Seat of the Pants*:

Explorer—mining the resources of the world

Artist—creatively presenting ideas

Judge—critique and refinement of presentations

Warrior—broadly advocating the positions

The climate for thinking skills to flourish is one where students can communicate freely. It is a safe place for each to exercise freedom of thought, where everyone's ideas are treated with respect and where students encourage each other to work out their ideas, no matter how fleeting they are. Students will develop their proficiency in thinking skills in a setting that could be perceived as a miniature think tank where good habits of mind become well-established early.

The social setting may let students know that all elements of critical thought—interpretations, questioning, trying possibilities, demanding rational justifications—are socially valued. The social setting may help to shape a disposition to engage in thinking. . . . We can expect intellectual dispositions to arise from long-term participation in social communities that establish expectations for certain kinds of behavior. Through participation in communities, students would come to expect thinking all the time, to view themselves as able, even obligated, to engage in critical analysis and problem solving.

(Lauren B. Resnick and Leopold E. Klopfer, *Toward the Thinking Curriculum: 1989 ASCD Yearbook*, p. 9)

Progressive Programs Used in Traditional Schools

Matthew Lipman's philosophy for children follows Jerome Bruner's tenet that any concept can be taught to children of any age as long as it is couched in a way that can be understood. Lipman has successfully introduced formal philosophical thought at the third grade level. His goal is to create a community of inquirers. He has accomplished this through cleverly-written novels which are read aloud, becoming the subject of student discussions focusing on human issues where clear reasoning and logic play an important role. Given ample training in the basics of rational thought processes, children have demonstrated the ability to reason through sticky interpersonal problems as well as complex issues.

In schools where self-initiated instruction is the prime mode for student learning, there will be more discourse among students on issues surrounding topics they are investigating, and there will be more written by students and teams supporting hypotheses and arguments they are making on behalf of the work they are undertaking. It is here that Lipman's approach can make a major contribution. It is in such a setting that Lipman's community of inquiry fits so well:

> We can now speak of "converting the classroom into a community of inquiry" in which students listen to one another with respect, build on one another's ideas, challenge one another to supply reasons for otherwise unsupported opinions, assist each other in drawing inferences from what has been said, and seek to identify one another's assumptions.
> (*Thinking in Education*, p. 15)

This complements very eloquently Leakey's observation that it is the complex social life of humans that makes us so intelligent.

Carla Beachy, a Maryland middle school teacher, uses an approach similar to Lipman's, in which books of social import become the focal point of group analysis, discussion, and presentations, using graphic organizers, thinktrix, and thinklinks as organizing principles. Her students are given many opportunities during the school year to practice these models, eventually gaining sufficient facility in their use to draw on them as a resource whenever appropriate.

Carol Schlichter has created a thinking-skills program, Talents Unlimited, based on Calvin Taylor's premise that every child has some talent at which she or he excels, as well as other talents which need to be refined. The program focuses on six areas: academics, productive thinking, planning, communication, forecasting and decision-making.

With continued analysis, some dimensions of these programs—all of which were formulated for traditional school use—could be adapted for the self-initiated learning environment as well.

Once you have equipped students with skills of inquiry, problem-solving, decision-making, forecasting, they are freed from dependency on their teachers in order to learn. They become free-thinking human beings, capable of looking at issues from all perspectives, aware of their biases, able to present arguments objectively, with clear logic and reasoning. After twelve years spent practicing these skills in a model social environment, they grow into mature, self-confident, socially responsible human beings ready to make significant contributions to the world in which they live.

Empowering masses of students to think clearly and constructively will have certain consequences. Colleges and universities will finally have to change their archaic ways of teaching, as most high school graduates will have already surpassed traditional undergraduate levels of study and will be well equipped to engage in a tutorial form of higher education. The non-college-bound graduate will be fully prepared to step directly into the decision-making positions which industry now characterizes as its greatest need. Many of these students will choose to set out on their own ventures, from launching new businesses to initiating unique ways of tackling great social issues of their time. Through divergent thinking and advanced negotiating skills, they will have already become experts in problem solving.

One of the central tenets of this book is that children must become seekers of knowledge before they can be fully educated, and this can only take place in a free learning environment. This also requires teachers who are truly knowledgeable in all dimensions of thinking skills and adept at labeling and shaping student behavior. To bring this about, we need to mount an effort similar to that which has been used to define thinking skills, and discover the best means to teach our teachers to be effective shapers of thinking-skill behavior. To support thinking-skill development, teachers must be aware of the consequences of every interaction with their students.

Children must be given ample opportunity to practice and refine these thinking skills until they are part of their very being. Parents and teachers alike will have to work hard to reorient their own thinking skills to respond to children's natural inquiry skills. Learning to turn a child's question back onto itself requires deliberate practice. We must learn to think first before being manipulated by a child into giving a quick answer.

The goal of thinking skills is to better equip our children to become effective world citizens, able to use their minds, rather than their emotions, when dealing with consequential issues.

There is something about the social interactive nature of thinking skills exploration that is itself stimulating, both to the mind and in terms of stimulating engagement and personnel commitment. A child who has well-honed thinking skills will have a competitive edge over those who do not. This thinking child/adult will be empowered to more fully cope with the complex issues of the twenty-first century.

Chapter 8
Creativeness vs. Destructiveness

Rule 4: Enable students to explore varied avenues of creativity and encourage them to develop proficiency in at least one.

Helping a child to discover key areas of creative potential, then allowing time and resources for their refinement, will go a long way toward helping to shape a fully-developed human being. Living a fulfilling life that draws upon one's inner resources of creativity and humanity will do much to counter the negative potential of using one's creativity for destructive purposes. We have many examples in our society of how destructive our youth can be. We have failed our children by not empowering them to discover their true creative potentials.

Early on in his enchanting fable *The Little Prince*, Antoine de Saint-Exupéry expresses the frustration children feel when adults fail to recognize the depths of their imagination:

The grown-ups' response, this time, was to advise me to lay aside my drawings of boa constrictors, whether from the inside or the outside, and devote myself instead to geography, history, arithmetic and grammar. That is why, at the age of six, I gave up what might have been a magnificent career as a painter. I had been disheartened by the failure of my Drawing Number One and my Drawing Number Two. Grown-ups never understand anything by themselves, and it is tiresome for children to be always and forever explaining things to them. (P. 4)

Helping children discover key areas of creative potential, then allowing them the time and resources to refine these areas, is an essential part of shaping fully-developed human beings. When children draw upon their inner resources of creativity to live fulfilling lives, they are less inclined to turn their creativity toward destructive purposes.

Erich Fromm opened my eyes to the importance of helping students develop their creative potential. Before I began this quest, I could not see the justification for the time students spend on creative pursuits. Activities like working with clay, painting, woodworking all appeared too remote from the rigor of disciplined study to qualify for the energy and attention children give them. This diversion from rigorous academics was an affront to my German heritage. I assumed as well that the sight of children playing around with arts-and-craftsy things would cause any casual observer to devalue the entire learning environment.

Then I read Fromm's essential thoughts on creativeness versus destructiveness in *The Sane Society*:

Another aspect of the human situation, closely connected with the need for relatedness, is man's situation as a creature, and his need to transcend this very state of the passive creature. Man is thrown into this world without his knowledge, consent or will. In this respect he is not different from the animal, from the plants, or from inorganic matter. But being endowed with reason and imagination, he cannot be content with the passive role of the creature, with the role of dice cast out of a cup. He is driven by the urge to transcend the role of the creature, the accidentalness and passivity of his existence, by becoming a "creator."

Man can create life. This is the miraculous quality which he indeed shares with all living beings, but with the difference that he alone is aware of being created and of being a creator. Man can create life, or rather, woman can create life, by giving birth to a child, and by caring for the child until it is sufficiently grown to take care of its own needs. Man—man and woman—can create by planting seeds, by producing material objects, by creating art, by creating ideas, by loving one another. In the act of creation man transcends himself as a creature, raises himself beyond the passivity and accidentalness of his existence into the realm of purposefulness and freedom. In man's need for transcendence lies one of the roots for love, as well as for art, religion and material production.

To create presupposes activity and care. It presupposes love for that which one creates. How then does man solve the problem of transcending himself, if he is not capable of creating, if he cannot love? There is another answer to this need for transcendence: if I cannot create life, I can destroy it. To destroy life makes me also transcend it. Indeed, that man can destroy life is just as miraculous a feat as that he can create it, for life is the miracle, the inexplicable. In the act of destruction, man sets himself above life; he transcends himself as a creature. Thus, the ultimate choice for man, inasmuch as he is driven to transcend himself, is to create or to destroy, to love or to hate. The enormous power of the will for destruction which we see in the history of man, and which we have witnessed so frightfully in our own time, is rooted in the nature of man, just as the drive to create is rooted in it. To say that man is capable of developing his primary potentiality for love and reason does not imply the naive belief in man's goodness. Destructiveness is a secondary potentiality, rooted in the very existence of man, and having the same intensity and power as any passion can have. But—and this is the essential point of my argument—it is only the alternative to creativeness. Creation and destruction, love and hate, are not two instincts which exist independently. They are both answers to the same need for transcendence, and the will to destroy must rise when the will to create cannot be satisfied. However, the satisfaction of the need to create leads to happiness; destructiveness to suffering, most of all, for the destroyer himself. (Pp. 36–38)

Consider Fromm's basic tenet:

> . . . *the will to destroy must rise when the will to create cannot be satisfied.*

This is a frightening thought. To me, it explains a great deal about the negative aspects of human behavior.

Within this quotation lies a basis for the elemental changes we must consider as we redesign our schools for the inquiring minds of the twenty-first century.

After reading Fromm, with my mind more in tune to the value of nurturing the creative dimension of human development, I was ready to receive with an open embrace an article by R. Craig Sautter which appeared in the *Phi Beta Kappan.*

In "An Arts Education School Reform Strategy," Sautter writes about using the arts to motivate and instruct students. He suggests that "education in and through the arts can play a significant role in changing the agenda, environment, methods, and effectiveness of ordinary elementary and secondary schools." Properly integrated into a creative school design, he argues, the arts become a potent force for developing "the thinking and imaginative abilities of students as they explore and learn about their world." (P. 433) Describing a form of education which parallels much of what I have written in this book, Sautter expands by saying that

The arts-integrated school . . . encourages students to learn in as many artistic and creative ways as they can imagine. . . . [It] seeks to stimulate young people to investigate many ways of knowing and many kinds of human experience . . . [and] puts a premium on the development of student imagination, thinking, feeling and communicating. Direct involvement in learning various art forms can help give students new and rich languages of expression. The arts can open them to the entire range of human history and cultural knowledge. Then, as an interdisciplinary tool, the arts can serve as an instrument for acquiring knowledge in other key areas, from reading and writing to mathematics and social science. (Ibid., p. 434)

Moreover, students learn the lessons of self-discipline, experience the rewards of hard work, and enjoy the benefits of working with others. Arts instruction teaches them about themselves, their sensations, and their ideas and shows them unexpected ways of understanding other people and the world.

> The arts promote the "hidden curriculum" of social behavior to improve self-discipline, self-motivation, self-esteem and social interaction. . . . The most frequently mentioned benefits of involvement in the arts came from the social interaction and camaraderie that develops in an arts group or activity. . . . Students in the arts learned to take criticism from peers, teachers, parents, and audiences. The constructive use of criticism . . . built confidence in at-risk students. It helped the students come to value themselves and their achievements. . . .
>
> . . . The strategy seeks to replace instructional methods that dissipate or repress the abundant energy and excitement of students; to introduce techniques that build on the social ties between students; to probe students' ideas, feelings, hypotheses, and visions; and to give them new languages of expression and thought. . . .
>
> . . . Since children and teenagers get such personal satisfaction from arts participation, the very atmosphere of an arts-integrated school is different from that of the traditional school. A genuine excitement and optimism pervades arts-integrated schools because students and teachers are vigorously involved in creating, practicing and performing. (Ibid., pp. 436–437)

What a contrast there is between Sautter's arts-integrated school and the traditional classroom, where students give up their freedom and consequently lose their sense of human dignity. Sautter's article shows yet again that it is possible to create a learning environment that empowers the child and nurtures the hungry mind. What amazes me is that when one really seeks these rich, empowering learning centers, they are to be found. I am truly dismayed that traditionalists cling so tenaciously to their top-down, fill-the-empty-vessel model, causing students a great amount of pain, when proven models exist today that can make learning so much more enriching for students.

Children come to school with a predisposition. Some come with a positive attitude—good inquiry skills, helpful disposition—while others arrive with a chip on their shoulders, with a need to prove themselves.

This predisposition is malleable. A series of punitive teachers could turn the child with a positive disposition into one who is always defensive. Effective teachers could build on the positive disposition and begin to turn the head of the child with a negative set. It is up to the teacher to find and build upon that single talent a child may have that will enable him to glow in his own eyes and in the eyes of his classmates. Being creative is a matter of talent development.

Something happens to students when you give them an opportunity to seriously explore and develop their potential creative talents. Another example, created literally a world apart from Sautter's arts-integrated school, speaks to the effect that in-depth, long-term involvement in refining a creative skill has on both the creative behavior of the students and their associated academic achievements.

Written in New Zealand in the mid-sixties, Elwyn Richardson's book *In the Early World* has long been a favorite of mine. Richardson explains in great detail how he created an arts-integrated school, even before the term had been invented, working with the most rural of children in a one-room schoolhouse in the northwesternmost corner of New Zealand.

The beauty of Richardson's book is that he tells how he went about creating the enriched learning environment, how the students responded, and most importantly, he includes many examples of the children's productions in art, prose, and poetry. The unfolding of these children's imagination and the opening of their eyes is evident in their breathtaking choice of words:

> At the beginning of my attempts to bring out creative thinking I was worried because the work appeared so much poorer than the writings the children had produced when I was using formal methods of teaching. But after only a few weeks I felt sure that the more creative methods produced better work than I could have obtained from a more formal approach. The informal creative writing is the measure of the writer's real ability, and I thought that the criticism and encouragement of this was more likely to be related to the individual's growth than set lessons. . . .
>
> . . . Rosalie's story about the hawk "flying on one wing" was the sort of thing that I was pleased to see others appreciated, for it had the same clarity of expression that I recognized from the stories the children were telling each other.
>
> Jennifer wrote about seeing a hawk from the barn window and "opening the door like a whispering sound". In all stories there appeared to be a working out of ideas and experiences rather than the writing of a specific story or poem. This working out of ideas was more characteristic of certain children, such as David W. "As the hawks glide side by side, their wings look raw, I don't know why . . . I know why. It's because he's high up in the air. I can see two of their heads looking down on us with their curved beaks looking down too, to see if I am going to shoot at them."

This piece of work had engaged a few children for about two hours. . . .

As can be seen, the writing tended to persist around a particular topic until interest had been satisfied. In many instances the interest began with an actual experience. . . . Interest was not always immediate, but tended to build up over a few weeks, as did the amount of work done. . . . Free time for writing is still the most requested period at the day's planning time. . . .

. . . Almost without exception the children were writing, reading, thinking, and talking about things they knew in their environment and in which they were genuinely interested. . . .

The wide range of writings done was in most cases coupled with some form of illustrative expression in the arts. This does not mean that the writing was considered to be the most important expression nor that the illustration was an afterthought. David was the initiator of all the work on hawks, but he wrote his few comments at the end. His mime dance of two hawks was far more important to him. I saw that some children, such as Derek and Mike, consistently did work that we all admired and commended, and this work was mainly painting. During discussions that we had on the set of hawk paintings, on the mime dance, the poetry, and the prose writings, Derek observed that often he painted things that he didn't mention in his story. In many cases children expressed their thoughts and apperceptions in visual art or drama before they did so in words.

Other children remarked that painting was an opportunity to reconsider thoughts or even go back to the original experience and that this allowed them to realize their purposes more clearly. (Pp. 72–75)

Richardson is not presenting a how-to-do-it book, but he does talk of failures—dead ends and plateaus in the children's development during which he was inclined to give up—as well as successes, for when he persisted he found the children breaking into new heights. He, too, discusses how children learn to accept criticism and learn how to critique classmates' work in a manner that shows great sensitivity to the nature of such comments.

All three of these works—Fromm's, Sautter's, and Richardson's—provide a sound argument for including in all twenty-first century schools an integral component that fosters students' creative talents. This may be the one element that will help trigger a student's enthusiasm for serious learning. This emphasis really becomes the core of the academic program. And it has to do with activating the total immersion of the self in learning.

However, I do not intend to imply that creativity thrives only within the arts. It is in the very nature of science that its progress depends on highly-creative people working intently—focused on solving problems with which they have become personally involved. At the bottom line, for these schools to be effective there must be multiple opportunities for students to have extended hands-on experience with projects that facilitate and expand their skills and knowledge no matter what their field of interest. This project orientation, which combines all of one's skills of inquiry, thinking, communicating—oral and written, interpersonal skills and hands-on experiences—lies at the heart of our future learning environment.

Learning Efficiency

How do you justify taking time away from children's academic studies and devoting it instead to helping them discover their creative potential?

The answer is obvious, at least to me. Once a child has found his life's love, he's halfway home.

And besides that, we do not need to keep our children's noses to the grindstone all day long. We only need to ensure that the time they do spend on their academic study is spent in an efficient manner. The proficiency of the learning experience, rather than the time invested, is what counts.

Two experiences have helped me to understand this. The first came one fall day on the waterfront in Annapolis, Maryland, as I watched two preteen girls scramble over the quarry wall into a dinghy, cast off, and set out rowing in a purposeful way—they were heading for a boat anchored in the harbor.

My first reaction was to intercede, to offer adult supervision and assistance. Luckily, I held my tongue. And observing their proficiency, I realized they were perfectly competent and needed no adult intervention.

These two girls had met the previous winter while their families were anchored at Georgetown in the Great Exhuma Islands of the Bahamas. One family was from Canada, the other from the Maine coast, and both had left jobs and homes behind for a year of sailing. For four months, the daughters studied together each morning for three hours and spent the remainder of their time exploring the harbor, the shoreline, and the island.

They hadn't seen each other since March, and it was now October. Their year on the water nearly over, both dreaded returning to school where they would be held captive for six or more hours a day—if they could keep up with all of their studies in three hours a day at sea, why should they have to spend so much time in school? It would be so boring!

But they did return to school, and they adjusted. More to the point, both were up to or beyond their classmates academically.

The second story comes from a National Geographic television program about several families living in the wilderness of Alaska, forty or fifty miles from their nearest neighbor. The children were visited occasionally by teachers who brought them self-study materials. These children, with no more than three hours a day at the books, achieved above-average scores on their SATs and become superior students in college.

I mention this to assuage the fears of parents and teachers who think that their children will not keep up with those in traditional classrooms if, in the self-initiated learning environment, we allow them more freedom than we are used to seeing.

In so doing, though, we allow joy, happiness, and enthusiasm to creep into the classroom. If the exploration of clay, wood, or painting is appropriately orchestrated by the teacher, other exciting things begin to happen: skills develop for which children can take pride, from which they can realize a sense of identity and self-esteem.

Creative skills have a value beyond knowledge. When one is knowledgeable, one can name the capitals of the world or the principles of physics. Skill comes into play while shaping amorphous clay into a beautiful pot, selecting the right colors to paint a sunset, the right keys and the proper tempo to play a piano concerto with feeling, the right timbers to build a boat.

To create is to develop and use skills and talents in a unique combination that distinguishes one individual from another. Groups of individuals can compete for a limited number of A's in school, which simply indicates their having equal or similar knowledge in a subject domain. Thus they have demonstrated their ability to acquire information.

Even in creative activities, one can either respond to an external demand, as when a teacher requires students to write a five-hundred-word essay or to complete fifty math problems in a workbook, or one can respond through self-initiation, as when a student is moved to write a descriptive essay on a particular experience, or to create a painting from a particular frame of reference.

Consider again Fromm's insight into the creative/destructive nature of human beings, and its relevance to the construction of the open/progressive classroom: *Children who are able to develop their creative potential fully are less likely to use their capacities in a destructive way.*

Someone might say, "He's a creative person," simply because that person did something beyond the skill level of the observer. But this is perceived creativity, which is not the creativity of which Fromm is speaking. The truly creative person has a well-honed talent from which he can claim an identity, a personal pride, a sense of accomplishment, an increased self esteem.

This end product, whether it be a dance, a painting, a book, or a boat, exists in two dimensions: first, in its pure form, it is a gift to humanity. Second, it becomes part of one's personal identity. The person who creates knows who he is; he has extended himself, has in some constructive way left a positive mark on humanity—added to the culture in which he lives.

The converse of this is Fromm's destructiveness, with the ultimate form being the taking of life. We do not have to look far to find examples. Simply turn on the news any evening of the week and you can see how we celebrate death. Our culture is fascinated with it.

Such destructiveness is not limited to destroying life; we also see destruction as gangs hijack cars just for the kick, or as extremist factions plant bombs to destroy great works of art.

These are all acts of individuals and groups existing on the outside of the community, who have not had an opportunity to find their own inner talents, nor an opportunity to develop their personal resources.

It is an interesting idea to think about. Consider a student who hasn't learned to express himself within the dimensions for which credit is given in school. His initial destructive tendency may simply be pigging out on junk food. From there it's not too hard to imagine this child pursuing the route of self-destruction to alcohol, illegal drugs, selling drugs to sustain his habits, and on to guns and killing others and eventually being killed.

All students who do not successfully develop their own creativity will not regress to this extreme of destructiveness. Many will stop with low self-esteem, becoming couch potatoes and watching television for seven hours a day or more.

In looking at this powerful idea of Fromm's, I immediately see a continuum, with our children's inactivity at the dead center. How often have you heard your child, or even yourself as a youngster, say, "There's nothing to do"? Ah yes, the perennial lament of summer vacation. . . . I believe that children's inability to motivate themselves to some creative end is the direct result of the educational system we have sustained for the past 150 years. That is what makes Fromm's idea so interesting. For me at least, it helps to justify those open/progressive classroom activities that seem so distant from academic learning.

A narrow perception of what constitutes true academics grows out of the Horace Mann approach to education. But now Erich Fromm has given me an insight into and justification for children messing about in clay and other two- and three-dimensional art forms. Consider that all of the symbols which we use for communication—printed words, spoken words, numbers—are representational abstractions of objects and ideas. We have learned that children gain a greater understanding of math and basic arithmetic through concrete objects called manipulatives. Give a child something as simple as bottle caps to work with, and suddenly it becomes clear what is meant by the equation $5 - 3 = 2$. Allowing ample time with concrete objects, the child gains a fuller and deeper understanding of the abstract symbols. Instead of just memorizing the multiplication tables, children discover the repetitive patterns that occur in sequence, resulting in a far more complete conceptualization of multiplication.

That is all understandable for math, but what does clay or art or woodworking or dramatic play or dance or music have to do with learning? Elwyn Richardson's account shows how the creative process in young children evolves into a concern for others, how the insights of one child may become a model for younger children, and how he led his students to express their feelings about their own work and the work of others. Working with objects the children had created in clay, Richardson modeled techniques that would later be used in writing. He helped the children to see details and then to express their ideas about details of their own and their classmates' work. Not only were evaluations of what was appealing expressed, but the children learned to fully express what aspects of a creation went into them. This attention to detail, looking for the beauty of objects and the representational nature of observation, led naturally to writing experiences in prose and poetry. Through these experiences, the children's sense of self-worth grew over time.

With a foundation of such creative experiences, do you think these children will be drawn toward the other end of Fromm's continuum—that of destructiveness?

Compare this with the experiences of children in traditional classrooms, and maybe you will begin to understand the frustration that they face. Deep down, each child has great potential. Our present system of education, which forces children into very rigid forms of learning, does not allow that potential to surface. New ideas, creative ideas are very delicate—flighty things. They have to be carefully nurtured—they cannot be forced into predetermined molds. A created object may be for the most part ugly, with a single aspect of beauty. With encouragement, the child will elaborate on the beautiful dimension until over time the object is deemed worth preserving. This is true of art, and is equally true of writing.

These new beginnings become the basis for habits of mind which enable children to reach out and probe deeply into other areas of interest. In addition to gaining self-esteem, they are learning what it takes to fashion products of quality through long-term attending skills, highly-focused behavior, critical evaluation, revision, and the refining of ideas. Little of this exists in the traditional classroom.

Fromm's is a profound statement—gives one a new insight into the intricacies of human nature, a new perspective on the destructiveness that exists in our inner cities and beyond. Consider this destructiveness combined with the human need for community, and you will have gone a long way toward understanding the dynamics underlying the behavior of troubled inner-city youths.

This may not represent a finding confirmed by cognitive psychologists or educational researchers, but it deserves as much or more attention than that given to some recent research findings. Depriving children of their opportunity to create may well be the condition that motivates them to explore their destructive potentials.

I will provide you with only one example of the lifelong effects that can come of assisting a child to develop a creative potential. In fact, I will introduce you to two adults—no longer children, high achievers, employed in challenging and stressful jobs. Joanne and Jim are married, in their mid- to late-thirties. Each has learned to play the piano well, each enjoys sitting at the keyboard and playing for an hour or so simply for relaxation. Joanne told me once that she looks forward to beating Jim home from work so that she can get to the piano before he does. All of the day's stress fades as she pours her emotions into the piece she is playing. Obviously, Jim uses his time at the piano for the same reason.

Now, after the music and a glass of wine, they are able to enjoy each other's company, sharing the experiences of the day or whatever they choose to talk about without the pressing stress clouding their intimacies.

The instrument of release does not have to be a piano. It can as easily be gardening, woodworking or, for that matter, any other creative leisure activity, such as whittling miniature totem poles, which one Maryland school principal is helping some of his students learn. If we don't provide children with an opportunity to explore their creative potentials, then we are depriving them of an important human dimension, and we as a society may have to contend with our youth exploring their destructive potentials instead.

Some students may even be lucky enough to discover and refine a creative talent that becomes a lifelong pursuit. In an eastern Long Island resort town, an art gallery decided to fill the void of a wintery February by inviting the local schools to display their students' best artwork. The display was so successful and the work was of such a high caliber, the director of the gallery reported that she could have sold thirty thousand dollars worth of art the first night.

What a marvelous way to celebrate the efforts of the most talented students. It is like a science fair for art students. We do this all the time within our schools, but it's another matter to recognize the very best through hanging in a real art gallery.

If we were to wait for scientific confirmation of every new idea, we would never be able to make an intuitive leap. Whether or not there are scientific studies to back up these ideas, I see this dimension of creativeness as an essential part of the reform we must enact in our schools. If we are to begin developing fully-educated human beings, we cannot overlook any dimension that helps to distinguish us as humans. Creativity is a very human trait. We are the only species that has sufficient self-awareness to be creative and likewise need to be so.

We as humans are never content with the status quo. We no sooner reach one plateau than we are striving for another. All too often, we realize the emptiness of our plateaus only after we attain them, at which point we begin to search for life's meaning. This is amply supported in media reports. It is also the reason that Thomas H. Naylor of Duke University's Business School has an oversubscribed course on Life's Meaning.

Our schools have focused on providing students with sufficient skills to earn a decent living. Not too bad a goal for the early twentieth century, as we moved from an agrarian society into the industrial age.

We now need to work on evolving an educational system that enables students to develop one or more of the creative potentials that exist in each of us.

Part 3
Application

Chapter 9
A brief picture of a rule-based classroom

Chapter 10
Relating self-initiated learning to current trends
Final thoughts

Chapter 9
Nurturing the Hungry Mind

The rule-based classroom is designed to help children retain their skills as natural inquirers in a more formal scholarly setting. Many authors have pointed out that preschool children have an insatiable appetite for learning. If you were to step back for some time and observe them at play, you would begin to see how they try on new roles and explore their environment. We as professional educators have to learn much more about how to recognize these natural inquiry skills and help children hone them. A child's quest for knowledge is a natural gift. We must respect it and nurture it.

In the past five chapters, I have described the environment in which the cultural and social aspects of a child's life can be developed and defined the four rules for enabling a child to learn throughout life. By doing this, we encourage our children to become focused, self-motivated, and reflective in their thinking, as well as creative in their actions.

As we begin to implement this school that is designed to empower the child, we must keep foremost in our minds the four dimensions of self-development that have emerged so far. These are the ability to initiate a project, the ability to remain focused on that project for long periods of time, the ability to think rationally and effectively, and the ability to discover and develop creative potential. As we begin the task of encouraging our children, providing them with the tools for knowledge acquisition and for reflective thought, we are also providing an environment and community that permits them to try out and refine their newly-acquired and integrated knowledge within a safe setting. This community further allows them to refine social interactive skills. Thus we have developed the potential for a community of inquiry, of interpersonal skills, and finally of *inner*personal skills, by empowering the child to develop creative potentials.

The big question now is, how do you nurture the hungry mind? A portion of the answer will be found in the many schools around the U.S. and the world that have already recognized and perfected this way of guiding students in their insatiable quest for knowledge. These are the schools that have become a home for the Justins of our country, who meet their teachers when they arrive in the morning and have to be sent home as the building is locked in the evening.

Another portion of the answer will be found in the children themselves. The very act of nurturing means to cultivate something that already exists. One nurtures a plant by giving it warmth, light, water, and food. A mother nurtures an infant in almost the same way. We cannot impose a curriculum on a young mind; instead, we must feed the mind with enabling skills that empower it to grow on its own.

Teachers need to know more about the minds of their students before they can begin to nurture them. It is here, at the very beginning, that this form of education splits from the traditional form. Traditionalists already know what they are going to do for these students before they ever meet them. Nurturing teachers can only devise their plans for guiding the children after they have met them and come to know their interests. Only then can the teacher/guide begin to help the children explore those interests.

Yet we cannot stop with encouraging only those interests a child brings to the classroom. Here we gain insight and guidance again from Caroline Pratt's book *I Learn from Children*, in which she stresses expanding the child's view of the world through first-hand experiences. Today, this broadening of personal experience is made available to increasing numbers of children through the Outward Bound network, which is reaching out to schools to broaden students' experiential learning. Pratt believed so strongly that students must gain first-hand experiences before they began to read that she delayed the introduction of reading until well into the second grade. Reading about something lacks the impact of experiencing it. Only pure experience involves all of the senses. In Pratt's classroom, these experiences are brought back to the school and played out, in what may be seen as a first level of abstraction, by—for example—building block representations of what the children have seen on a trip to the waterfront of New York City.

As the children begin to play out the roles of people they have seen on their outings, they try on various life roles and interpersonal relationships. In this way, Pratt provides her students with a common experience they can use to expand on their personal experiences. When they return to the classroom, they turn to drawing, clay, or other media to make representations of their experiences, and they then attach words to these representations. They are learning a great deal about how to transpose rich experiences into words, forming a basis for writing, which in turn helps the children grasp how to decode words and thus learn fully how to read. The wise teacher will use this technique to show students of different backgrounds how they can view a shared experience from different perspectives, where some students see details totally overlooked by others.

A program developed at the University of New Hampshire, Image-Making Within the Writing Process, demonstrates this encoding process by teaching children to make beautiful textured paper and use it to create collages representing their experiences. There is some quality within the abstractness and colorfulness of the handmade papers that helps to elicit powerful descriptive words. This is illustrated in Beth Olshansky's essay *David's Journey* which begins on page 113.

Having Faith in Students and Teachers

If this system is to work, we must have faith in our teachers' ability to adapt, and in our children's ability to inquire and learn. This is the antithesis of our current system, in which we rely on research findings and scientific methods to test hypotheses. Under such a structure, we cannot alter the way we teach without having the changes first proven through rigorous research.

David's Journey:
Image-Making Within the Writing Process
Beth Olshansky

David is an eight-year-old student with an attention deficit problem. If you are looking for David in the classroom, you soon learn not to look for him at his desk for he is rarely in his seat. Writing time is the worst for David. In his own words, "I hate to write. The words fly out of my head before I can get them down on paper." David spends much of writing time each day sharpening and re-sharpening his pencil, getting drinks at the water fountain, and finding a variety of other excuses to wander around the room. In two months time he managed to produce two sentences of writing, only under the threat of not going out to recess if he did not write something. David loves recess. Each day he waits for recess to arrive where he is free to run and play without the glaring eyes of his teacher piercing him. Sadly, by the second grade, David has already learned that teachers do not take kindly to him and that he is failing in school.

When David was first introduced to The Image-Making Process via the making of a variety of hand-painted textured papers, he did not stand out in the crowd. He moved from station to station, completely engaged in each art process. David even went back to the bubble print station to create a second round of bubble prints.

As the class viewed textured papers together, David did stand out from his peers, however, as one of the first children to discover images within the textured papers. Rich language and imaginative images were at the tip of his tongue.

When it came time for the children to begin their story-making process, David immediately "envisioned" his story. A geometric design in a plexi-glas print he had made reminded him of a window. He quickly cut it out and literally peered through it to discover the rest of his story. A big blue swirl in a textured paper became a blustery tornado and thick blue and purple bubble prints became ominous clouds. As a visual and kinesthetic learner (and a child who struggled with writing), David chose to make collage image after collage image, eagerly securing his ideas down on paper in pictures. Being an active child, his story-making process was very physical. His blue marbleized tornado literally spun through the air accompanied by great swishing sounds before he hastily fastened it to the page before it too blew away.

As David created each collage image, he was obviously re-hearsing his story over and over in his mind and would eagerly share it with any passer-by. His oral language was unusually rich and descriptive. As he traced the lines of each collage image with his active fingers, descriptive language was at the tip of his tongue. His language appeared to come directly off of his collage images. Holding an uncombed purple and magenta marbleized paper in his hand, he called out, "It feels like we are caught in a meteor shower. Huge rocks like pumpkins hit me from all sides. It's raining rocks." David ducked, his hands flying up over his head to protect him from the "dusty storm".

David retold his story so many times, that he had memorized it before he ever began to put words down on paper. This, plus the strong visual record of his thoughts in his own images, ensured that his words would no longer "fly out of his head."

David created both words and pictures. His published book was outstanding in both text and illustrations. After looking through his published book for the first time, David looked up and with tears in his eyes said, "I didn't know I could do that good."

The Horrified Tornado
by David

It's night and the wind is whipping. I'm looking out my strong window. The storm is getting closer. It gets quieter and quieter and smaller and smaller.

Then a tornado appears! It rocks around in circles through the clouds. Then it disappears!

More dark clouds come. Then hard rain comes, wild like a lion. Lightning strikes all of the houses but ours. The dusty wind comes and rocks fly all over the place.

It seems like we're caught in a meteor shower. I go outside. Huge rocks like pumpkins hit me from all sides. It's raining rocks.

It gets quieter. I peek out my window again. The air is brighter. The mighty storm is over.

I go back to sleep.

(*NDN Stories*, pp. 46–47)

And why shouldn't we have faith in our teachers' ability to make moment-to-moment decisions as they interact with their students? They have accumulated years of experience in the educational process. Many know intuitively what action is best at any given moment. Combining this experiential background with appropriate retraining, they will do well with students in self-initiated learning environments.

What might the impact be if we should believe in our students' innate ability to learn? Consider a teacher-student interaction. The student is questioning her own ability to accomplish a task. The teacher says, "You can do it! I have faith in your ability to complete this task. Now let's take it one small step at a time." And the child begins to gain faith in herself. Isn't this where self-confidence originates? As we begin to build faith in ourselves, we can learn to have faith in others. Faith has an empowering dimension to it. Associated with this faith is the concept of being a reliable person, and the concept of being relied on.

I also propose that we have faith in our children's ability to teach us the route to a higher order of learning. Their minds are open, they approach problems without preconceived solutions, they are extremely adaptable. If we loosen the reins, then they may show us the way. In order to do this well, we must have faith in ourselves—faith in our conviction that this bottom-up form of education is the way to truly empower the child.

Consider the top-down type of education practiced today, in which we force students into a preconceived curriculum that does not provide for initiative. Doesn't this disempower them as we force them into these molds?

Demonstrating our own faith in our children's ability to learn directly affects our ability to empower our children.

The Classroom Environment

The form of education I have been describing throughout this book works best in a classroom where one teacher interacts with about two dozen students—eight from each of three grade levels, such as kindergarten, first, and second or third, fourth, and fifth. Where funding allows, I suggest that children enter this learning environment at age two, or as soon as they are toilet-trained, yielding a preschool class that still includes three age groupings. The advantage of such a class lies in the continuity that is allowed; you would not want to have a child start preschool with one form of education only to be introduced to another when it came time to start public school.

Eight new students join the group each year, whom the teacher and the remaining sixteen students must befriend, get to know intimately, and work into the classroom routine. To make the new children feel welcome and comfortable, big sister and big brother relationships are encouraged, teaching the important social concept of caring for others. During their first weeks in the classroom, the new children spend part of their time looking over the shoulders of the older ones, learning by observing the processes in which they will soon be deeply engaged.

The school as a whole is rich in resources, many of them dictated by the interests of the students. Once well established, most students delve into interests that are common to children of this age in this culture. Although some resources are child-specific, many others are dictated by the need to have students engaged in activities that help them attain the basic skills. To that end, there are lots of manipulatives for learning basic math concepts. (Children have been known to go all the way up to basic concepts of calculus using manipulatives.) The same is true of science materials, but most of what the children learn comes through natural inquiry into topics of interest to them. This classroom may look like a cluttered and chaotic environment, yet the teacher is truly in charge of what materials are there for the children to explore, and each item has been chosen to help a child begin or continue on a course of inquiry.

Books are a key resource in this setting. Most—if not all—reading material is in the form of primary resources, as opposed to textbooks in which the subject matter has been selected and interpreted by the author. A well-stocked reference library is a necessity to support these children.

This is a cozy classroom, with niches and window seats where students can curl up with a good book or a pad and pencil and concentrate for long periods without interruption. This is where the rules for social behavior become so important. As they probe into something of great interest to them, the children learn the importance of focused behavior, which teaches them to respect each other's investigations. This does not mean the classroom must be quiet—a focused child will not even hear his name called—but it does mean that classmates cannot pester one another during a time of great concentration.

It is not for me to lay out all the exploratory dimensions of the school. The teacher is in charge, and yes, there are basic skills that all students will master, but it is not done in any lockstep fashion. The teacher makes it clear what her expectations are for each student. The students have the opportunity and the freedom to acquire basic skills at times when they are most relevant to other dimensions of their learning. This is an efficient means of skills acquisition, which results in a greater retention rate because the students attain the knowledge when it has meaning for them.

Teachers I have known are revitalized and energized by the enthusiasm for learning their students develop through self-initiated inquiry. Teachers find themselves able to work with each child at a level they have never before experienced. In such a setting, the teachers become true professionals, fully in charge of the learning environment. This is not true in the lockstep curriculum where, for instance, each teacher in every school in the county teaches math during the third period each day because research states that students learn math best in the morning just before lunch.

Some teachers question the added work, believing that self-initiated learning requires developing a lesson plan for each child every day for every subject. But this is an overstatement; in this environment, children draw up weekly contracts in consultation with their teacher for a major portion of their work. The self-directed child does most of this planning. The teacher's role is to guide the children in expanding their horizons and their point of view, both during the contract-planning stages and throughout the week as they forge ahead on their individual and group projects.

It is not all individually-initiated work, though. There are times for group experiences, times for sharing and critiquing each other's work, and times of celebrating accomplishments. And times for enriching small group and large group interactions.

Another phenomenon occurs in these open-ended learning environments: as students are encouraged to explore their interests to the fullest extent possible, some emerge as such experts that they become models and teachers for others. One student stands out in my mind who, while in first grade, progressed through fifth grade math. Others in the class who were having difficulty with math basics were paired with this expert and from his tutoring gained much ground in their math proficiency.

Although teachers in these settings have more freedom than traditional teachers, there are distinct standards to which they must adhere. One magnet school is permitted to exist with a hands-off policy as long as their students maintain reasonable scores on the district standardized testing program. In Maryland, these standards are set through a performance testing program where schools, not students, receive grades. The movement toward performance testing favors the behaviors that are being developed in schools emphasizing self-initiated learning. Performance tests are made up of items that represent authentic, real-world problems engaging not only individual students, but also teams of students working together to find solutions. Portfolio evaluations, which originated in progressive schools thirty-five years ago, are also gaining support as a means of assessing student achievement.

The defining difference in these schools lies in the creation of a learning environment in which a community/culture focuses on human development and personal growth, in which the individual students are ultimately responsible for their own education. When each student is a responsible party in a small-scale caring community, the spirit of personal freedom prevails.

It is not an easy task to set up and maintain such a learning environment. It is like living on the edge of chaos. It involves risk-taking. But there are those who contend that we only really learn when risks are taken. Keeping within safe bounds limits our experiences and, consequently, limits what we learn. I encourage you to come to the edge of chaos and learn with the children what life is really about. When you feel at a loss as to where to turn next, don't give up. Instead, look to the children and they will show you the way. You simply need to listen closely and you will hear the nuances of their clear voices. Nurture them! You will be amazed at how they grow.

Further Reading

Many authors and educators have written well about the day-to-day processes in the open/progressive classroom. Look to Roland Barth's *Open Education and the American School* for a good account of how this free learning environment manages through integrated instruction to cover all the basics included in traditional curricula and much more. Richardson's book, to which I have often referred, explains how day-to-day activities build over time, eventually producing rich language experiences as children evolve from discovering their own commitment, through learning, through the arts. In *The Hundred Languages of Children*, by Carolyn Edwards, Lella Gandini, and George Forman, several chapters discuss how children learn in the Reggio Emilia approach to early childhood education. The following insert from David Armington of Educational Development Center gives a brief but pointed summary of an environment conducive to nurturing the hungry mind. I would also recommend R. Craig Sautter's report to the MacArthur Foundation, *Creating Arts-Integrated Schools*.

A list of viable resources would be incomplete if they did not include the work of Howard Gardner and David Perkins at Harvard in Project Zero. This is a project-based instructional model that sees students as workers and teachers as coaches. It encourages students to learn to use knowledge to solve unexpected problems, rather than parrot back facts.

One should not overlook the work done by NAEYC in creating guidelines for developmentally appropriate practice for early childhood education. These guidelines are child-centered, learner-active collaborative approaches to educating children from birth through third grade.

Brain Compatible Learning Activities

from "A Plan for Continuing Growth"
by David Armington of the
Educational Development Center
in Newton, Massachusetts

1. There is a rich environment of materials for children to explore and there are abundant opportunities to learning through experience.

2. Children's responses to the environment provide many of the starting points for learning. Activities most often arise from the needs and interests of the group rather than from a prescribed curriculum. When commercial materials and programs are used, they must be made available in ways that protect the children's responsibility for their own learning.

3. With guidance from the teacher, children plan their own activities, drawing from a range of relevant choices.

4. Each child is free to explore an interest deeply and is also free to disengage when an activity no longer seems appropriate.

5. Typically, there are a variety of activities going on simultaneously, each child working in ways best suited to interests, talents, and style.

6. There are few obvious barriers between subjects and much of the child's work is, in fact, interdisciplinary.

7. There is minimum dictation by the clock. A flexible schedule permits children to learn according to their individual rhythms of engagement and disengagement.

8. The children talk with each other about their work and often work together. Their learning is frequently a cooperative enterprise marked by dialogue.

9. All forms of expressive representation in the arts and in movement, as well as in language, are considered valid and important.

10. Groupings are not based on fixed criteria such as age or reading level, but are kept flexible, shifting with the changing needs and interests of children.

11. The teacher serves in a supportive rather than a didactic role, guiding the children, provisioning and structuring the environment. Staff are sensitive observers and active participants in the life of the program.

Chapter 10
Relating Self-Initiated Learning to Current Trends in Education

In 1400, our youth was a poor peasant without identity, working the fields by day and sleeping on a flea-infested bed of straw at night. In 1900, our youth had just left the farm for a career in the big city and found himself instead performing a highly-repetitive job on a production line, ten hours a day, six days a week. In 1994, almost the twenty-first century, our youth is an independent consultant at age fifteen, making $95 an hour with two hundred clients clamoring for his expertise in computer programming and networking.

Scientists refer to the complex adaptive nature of man as a form of emergence. Certainly, it is clear from the brief six-hundred-year history of mankind above, that man's behavior has emerged from mere existence to a higher level of actuality. Emergence is the force that drives us to evolve, and our youth are out there at the edge, leading the way. If our schools are to empower them, if our schools are to contain them at all, then it is time for a dramatic change in the way we enable our youth to become educated.

The basic skills for the twenty-first century must be enabling skills. The old-fashioned skills of reading, writing, math, science, and social studies are too archaic and restrictive for our future schools. This is not to say that their content is unimportant, only that the means of acquiring this content are outmoded.

Right now, there are too many ideas of what constitutes a good education, and too many parents still opting for a system that reflects the way they were educated—a system that won't work for the twenty-first century. In this book, I have outlined a rule-based system of education. Could you call it a new philosophy of education? It is undoubtedly a different view of how children learn. It is clearly only a bare skeleton on which those who dare could build a powerful new system of education. It does need to be fleshed out. But I see this as the role of those communities that collectively decide to put the effort into making it work. It must truly be a community effort, involving every member—including the children. So much can be learned by carefully listening to their insights.

Self-initiated learning can flourish only if all parties are fully committed to its success. It requires that everyone agree on the same high standards and expectations for their children. The magnet school represents one way to work within the public sector, regrouping parents and students in order to attain this purposeful focus. Presently, the primary alternative is private schools, where there is an obvious selection process in place. Private schools have provided the setting in which progressive education has flourished over the years, and it is unfortunate that more parents and children haven't had the opportunity to participate in this intellectually-rich form of education.

The prospects are looking ever brighter for open/progressive education. Today I see multiple opportunities for communities to make the transition toward open/progressive education schools, and many schools are taking advantage of these opportunities. For example, a multi-year open classroom was launched in an East Hampton, New York elementary school in the fall of 1993. At Columbia University, the Coalition of Essential Schools at Brown, an alternative education project operating at the high school level, has implemented an elementary school offshoot called the Center for Collaborative Education. The Reggio Emilia Approach to Early Childhood Education has been recognized and respected among educators for some years now. Many of the New American School models contain open classroom components. It is as if the movement has been in people's minds for years, as it has been in mine, and suddenly everyone is speaking out at once.

The American Psychological Association has developed a set of specifications that enumerate how students learn best, which is now available from McREL. My interpretation of this publication is that it supports well my tenets of educating students in a rule-based environment versus traditional top-down programming. This document provides such a strong psychological basis for self-initiated learning that I have seriously considered publishing it in the appendix of this book.

In March 1993, the Association for Supervision and Curriculum Development (ASCD) celebrated its fiftieth anniversary with a convention focused on Creating Learning Communities. Keynote speaker Ernest Boyer, president of the Carnegie Foundation for the Advancement of Teaching, presented a list of student achievements and school outcomes for students of the twenty-first century, all of which would be readily attainable by students in progressive schools that apply self-initiated learning techniques. The educational trend is clearly moving away from the restrictive form introduced by Horace Mann 150 years ago.

I'd like to again return to the concept of phase change. The process of changing a substance like water from one state to another, e.g. ice to water. There are other phase changes of a dramatic nature, from conductor to super conductor, from non-magnetic to magnetic. In each case, tremendous amounts of energy are necessary to make the shift from one state to another. We are on the verge of a phase change, as the critical mass of dissatisfaction with our educational system reaches the point where such a change becomes inevitable. And I am hopeful that this change will be in the direction of rule-based education such as I have outlined in this book.

Look again at the influences:

if computer-generated birds can learn to fly and avoid objects,

if social interaction is the basis for intellectual growth,

if freedom is the basis for human dignity,

if creativity is the cure for destructiveness,

and

if the other rules of self-motivation, thinking, and focus prove valid,

then

don't we hold the keys to empowering the child of the twenty-first century through such a highly-charged educational experience?

I began this book with the notion that it is incomplete—a mere beginning attempt to define a new perspective on how children learn. This beginning needs the contributions of other minds, but as you consider additions or other variations, remember one basic rule: Keep it simple. A bottom-up, rule-based philosophy of education will founder and fail if you burden it with more rules than you can count on a single hand.

The astute reader will recognize that what I have presented here raises more questions than it answers. To attain those answers, the community must use the very process of inquiry I have proposed for their children—and in so doing, will experience first-hand the possibilities that are uncovered as one probes deeper and deeper into this form of education.

After Thoughts

When I started this book, I had no idea it would evolve as it has. Not in my wildest imaginings could I have predicted the combination of new insights this quest would bring me. The very act of writing has clarified vague ideas and provided new perspectives that leave me in awe of the writing process. I have long contended that I wished to write this book for myself, in order to coalesce my thoughts. It has done that and much more. I now view all of what I see changing in education from this new perspective.

I keep wanting to go back and refine the ideas in each chapter, but I am convinced each idea needs the debate of other minds. If they are of value, they will grow as others add their own insights. If not, the book will gather dust as so many thousands of others have done—a momentary experience only to be overshadowed by the next. I hope not. I see it as an initial framework for viewing more refined educational change as it emerges in the twenty-first century.

This writing experience has been for me like the emergence of new behavior as is so well discussed in the three books on complexity I have read. The very act has been the most revealing, profound experience of my life. I could have never imagined beforehand the content of each chapter. Each idea seemed to flow out of an inner warehouse I never before imagined existed. Even if no one accepts my ideas, I live with the fulfilling experience that has come with its creation.

Many people with whom I discussed this book have indicated their enthusiasm for the ideas I have tried to develop here, so I feel I can expect it to be read seriously by some, and accepted at some level; whether it evokes sufficient momentum to make a difference will have to be seen.

I am certain my ideas will generate some criticism. But before you cut away too deeply at the details, I ask you to consider the whole. The examples cited reflect the scope—and the limitations—of my own experience, viewing these programs in action.

One last note—if you are encouraged by this model, move slowly and purposefully. Don't let it be just another fad. Develop five- and ten-year plans. Create pilot programs and learn from small commitments, and finally, don't inflict it on everyone. Respect the rights of those who choose to stay with the tried and traditional methods.

Notes

Page

5   Waldrop, M. Mitchell. *Complexity.* P241.

9   Ibid. P. 229.

19   Covey, Stephen. *The 7 Habits of Highly Effective People.*
           Pp. 16–21.

19   Gibran, Kahlil, *The Prophet.* P 18.

23   *Coalition of Essential Schools*: Box 1969, Brown Uni-
           versity, Providence, RI 02912. (401) 863-3384

23   Covey, Stephen. *The 7 Habits of Highly Effective People.*
           Pp. 224–229.

27   This vignette was drawn from the author's visit to the
           Prospect School in Bennington, VT in the early seven-
           ties. Patricia F. Carini was the principal at that time.

29   This experimental school was established by the Pitts-
           burgh Board of Education in the early seventies for 60
           fourth and fifth grade students.

30   This vignette was drawn from a verbal description of the
           M-3 Project which originates at the University of Pitts-
           burgh's Learning Research and Development Center.

55   *Microfilmed the students' portfolios of one school for
           extended study* - Microfilmed portfolios of 36 students on
           microfiche and color slides who attended the Prospect

School over a 25-year period can be obtained from either the Prospect Archives, Center for Education & Research, P.O. Box 326, North Bennington, VT 05257, or the Center for Teaching and Learning at the University of North Dakota.

56   *City-as-School* - City-As-School is a National Diffusion Network alterative program that combines academic learning with the world of work for high school students, including at-risk students. Contact William Weinstein, City-As-School, 16 Clarkson Street, New York, NY 10014. (212) 645-6121, 691-7801.

62   Pratt, Caroline. *I Learn from Children.* Chapter 6, pp. 67-80, discusses the life of six-year-olds at school. The entire book is must reading for anyone considering this form of school.

80   *Higher Order Thinking Skills (HOTS)* - a National Diffusion Network program with alternative approach to Chapter 1 for grades 4-6 in which compensatory services consist solely of higher order thinking activities. Contact Stanley Pogrow or Christi Estrada, University of Arizona, College of Education, Tucson, AZ 85721. (602) 621-1305.

82   von Oech, Roger. *A Kick in the Seat of the Pants.* P. 14.

83   *Philosophy for Children* - a National Diffusion Network program that offers conceptual and cultural enrichment while providing skill improvement in comprehension, analysis, and problem solving. Specifically, the program develops reasoning competencies (e.g., inferring and finding underlying assumptions) and inquiry skills (e.g., forming hypotheses and explaining) for grades 3-7. Con-

tact Matthew Lipman, Professor of Philosophy and Director, Institute for the Advancement of Philosophy for Children, Montclair State College, Upper Montclair, NJ 07043. (201) 655-4277.

84   *Carla Beachy, a Maryland middle school teacher* - You may read about her work in "Enhancing Writing Through Cooperative Peer Editing," *Enhancing Thinking through Cooperative Learning*, Neil Davidson and Toni Worsham, eds. New York: Teachers College Press (1992). Pp. 209–220.

84   *graphic organizers, thinktrix and thinklinks as organizing principles* - thinking skills devices developed by Frank Lyman, Jr. See "Think-Pair-Share, Thinktrix, Thinklinks, and Weird Facts: An Interactive System for Cooperative Thinking," *Enhancing Thinking through Cooperative Learning*, Neil Davidson and Toni Worsham, eds. New York: Teachers College Press (1992). Pp. 169–181.

84   *Talents Unlimited* - a National Diffusion Network teacher training/learning model which integrates creative and critical thinking skills into the curriculum for grades 1-6. Contact Brenda Haskew, Talents Unlimited, 1107 Arlington Street, Mobile, AL 36605. (205) 690-8060.

111   *Outward Bound* - Expeditionary Learning Outward Bound USA, 122 Mount Auburn Street, Cambridge, MA 02138. (617) 576-1260.

112   *Image-Making Within the Writing Process* - a National Diffusion Network program that promotes literacy skills in elementary school-aged children through the integration of visual imagery throughout their writing process.

Contact Beth Olshansky, The Laboratory for Interactive Learning, University of New Hampshire, Hood House, 89 Main Street, Durham, NH 03824. (603) 862-2186.

119   *Portfolio evaluations, which originated in progressive schools* - see note above regarding page 53.

120   Project Zero Development Group, Harvard Graduate School of Education, 323 Longfellow Hall, Cambridge, MA 02138. (617) 495-1000.

121   NAEYC, National Association for the Education of Young Children, Order book number 224; Developmentally Appropriate Practices in Early Childhood Programs Serving Children from birth through age eight. Send $5.00 in check or money order to NAEYC, 1509 16th Street, Washington, DC 20036-1426 Attn: Resource Sales. (202) 232-8777.

127   *Center for Collaborative Education* - 1573 Madison Avenue, Room 201, New York, NY 10029. (212) 348-7821.

127   *New American School* - this is the organization established by President Bush and funded by USA corporations to provide grants to ten cutting edge model programs for school improvement. Three of the programs mentioned in this book have been funded from this source. They include the Coalition of Essential Schools, the Community Schools in Minneapolis-St. Paul and the Outward Bound project in Cambridge, Massachusetts. See the New American Schools Development Corporation, 1000 Wilson Boulevard, Suite 2710, Arlington, VA 22209. (703) 908-9500.

127   *American Psychological Association has developed a set of specifications that enumerate how students learn best, which is now available from McREL - Learner-Centered Psychological Principles: Guidelines for School Redesign and Reform.* Presidential APA Task Force on Psychology in Education (January 1993). $4.00. Contact the Mid-continent Regional Educational Laboratory (McREL), 2550 S. Parker Road, Suite 500, Aurora, CO 80014. (303) 337-0990.

127   *Association for Supervision and Curriculum Development (ASCD)* - Ernest Boyer gave the keynote address to the 1993 ASCD Convention, whose theme was Creating Learning Communities. One is able to purchase a copy of this address on audiotape from ASCD, 1250 N. Pitt Street, Alexandria, VA 22314. (703) 549-9110. $10.00.

Bibliography

Armington, David. *A Plan for Continuing Growth*. Newton, MA: Educational Development Center (1968).

Barth, Roland S. *Open Education and the American School*. New York: Agathon Press, Inc. (1972).

Covey, Stephen R. *The 7 Habits of Highly Effective People*. New York: Simon & Schuster (1990).

de Saint Exupéry, Antoine. *The Little Prince*. Orlando, FL: Harcourt Brace & Company (1971).

Edwards, Carolyn, Lella Gandini, and George Forman, eds. *The Hundred Languages of Children*. Norwood, NJ: Ablex Publishing Corp. (1994).

Fromm, Erich. *The Art of Loving*. New York: HarperCollins Publishers Inc. (1989).

Fromm, Erich. *The Sane Society*. New York: Henry Holt and Co., Inc. (1990).

Gibran, Kahlil. *The Prophet*. New York: Alfred A. Knopf (1993).

Hart, Leslie A. "Classrooms Are Killing Learning: A History of the Graded Classroom," *The Brain Based Education Networker* (Fall 1992): 2-3, 6.

Leakey, Richard & Lewin, Roger. *Origins Reconsidered: In Search of What Makes Us Human*. New York: Doubleday (1992).

Lipman, Matthew. *Thinking in Education.* New York: Cambridge University Press (1991).

May, Rollo. *Freedom and Destiny.* New York: W.W. Norton & Co., Inc. (1989).

Olshansky, Beth. "David's Journey: Image-Making Within the Writing Process," *NDN Stories* (February 1994): 46-47.

Pearce, Joseph Chilton. *The Magical Child.* New York: E. P. Dutton (1980).

Pratt, Caroline. *I Learn from Children.* New York: HarperCollins Publishers Inc. (1990).

Richardson, Elwyn S. *In the Early World.* New York: Random House (1964).

Sautter, R. Craig. "An Arts Education School Reform Strategy," in *Phi Delta Kappan* (February 1994): 433-434, 436-437.

Sautter, R. Craig. *Creating Arts-Integrated Schools: An Arts Education School Reform Strategy,* Working Draft, submitted to the John D. and Catherine T. MacArthur Foundation, November 13, 1992.

von Oech, Roger. *A Kick in the Seat of the Pants.* New York: HarperCollins Publishers Inc. (1986).

Waldrop, M. Mitchell. *Complexity.* New York: Simon & Schuster (1992).